Saving Our Daughters

From A Man's Point of View VOL.2

CURTIS J. BENJAMIN

Copyright © 2009: Curtis J. Benjamin
Cover | Layout Design: Eric M. Croas - Cat's Meow Communications
Creative Director/Agent for ICTBS Publishing: Mickala L. Williams -
micwms@lvlnxt.com
Publisher: ICTBS Publishing

ICTBS Publishing Editorial Team
Lead Editor - Eric M. Croas
Copy Editor - Tara Coyt - The Write Author Coach
Lead Contributor - Dr. Barbara Becker Holstein: Originator of THE ENCHANTED
SELF(r), Positive Psychologist and Happiness Coach and Author of The Truth
(I'm a girl , I'm smart and I know everything)

Other Contributors -
Veronica Bates
Harold David Hairston B.S., M.S., D.P.S., O.D.T
Tequilla Whitfield
Stacii Jae Johnson
Tracy Heffner

ICTBS thanks all contributors and celebrites for their contribution to the Saving
Our Daughters book series.

Library of Congress Control Number: 2008940628

Legal Services and Clearances provided by:
The Law Office of Omara S. Harris, Esq., LLC
P.O. Box 18771; Atlanta, GA. 31126

ADVERSITY

"Blessed are ye, when men shall hate you, when they shall separate you from their company, and shall reproach you, and cast out your name as evil, for the Son of man's sake."

~ Luke 6:22

"Another supporting scripture given by my mother to help guide and provide me strength through the troubles of this world."

~ Curtis J. Benjamin

~ TABLE OF CONTENTS ~

~ TABLE OF CONTENTS ~

ACT III
To Whom It May Concern
Reflections From The Women Of Saving Our Daughters

ENCORE
IN MEMORY OF...

Encourage her to be strong and to stand up for herself no matter what the circumstances are. Ignore the kids at school because if you feed into it they will continue to tease you. Whereas if you ignore them, they will move on to someone that gives them a reaction. As you raise your kids you have to teach them to love, respect and care for themselves and others.

~ Roger Bobb (Executive Producer of Tyler Perry Studios) with his darling daughter, Renee

OPENING MONOLOGUE

To The Reader:

As you will discover about the Saving Our Daughters book series, these books are like a "Talk Show in a Book." They offer women an insight to how men think when it comes to dealing with issues surrounding raising their daughters.

They also get to hear how these men feel about relationships and true family love. Readers will also read about intense emotional topics such as domestic violence; teen vs. teen abuse; effective communication between children and their parents; the discipline of our children; and advice for daughters about finding a positive male role model when the father is absent in the home and life.

A strong and highly heated new topic in this volume will be community self-esteem based upon the shade and color of our skin. Included in the discussions are self-hate based on the color of a man's skin tone; how interracial and bi-racial relationships can affect the family; teenagers facing prejudice amongst their peers based on the different shades of their skin; and the controversial "brown paper bag" test.

So dear reader, I welcome you to this installment of the Saving Our Daughters book series, and please enjoy your copy of this "Talk Show in a Book."

So where do we begin with this delicate subject of color and racism within a race -- I call it intra-racial profiling -- and how it affects our decisions, about all relationships, including how we choose our partners?

You may say that our second book has nothing to do with properly raising daughters and learning how to be positive fathers and men in our communities, but I beg to differ. We must first stop judging each other based on the color of our skin.

We must also stop making comments like, "I want to date outside of my race to have cute babies." When our children hear or see this, they begin to equate light skin tone with physical attractiveness and personal value. It doesn't help the situation when people make comments like, "Oh he or she looks good, to be dark skinned." WHAT DOES THAT MEAN PEOPLE?

When we call someone "Pretty Boy" in reference to an individual being light-skinned, why don't we ever say it about a person with a darker complexion?

These topics were last explored in Spike Lee's powerful and controversial films School Daze and Jungle Fever in the 80's/90's. Now we have decided to bring it back into our community's focus!!

These color distinctions are damaging our children, our people. As a dark-skinned male, I occasionally still have to deal with this sensitive topic myself.

As a young man I was scarred by the senseless jokes born out of stereotypes based on the shade of my skin. Through each of the men's interviews featured in this book, I grew and began to understand and heal.

Through my healing I became more empowered by the pride I have in my skin color. I want our children, regardless of their skin tone or racial makeup, to feel that same empowerment and pride.

Sincerely,

Curtis J. Benjamin

P.S.: My motivation for writing the Saving Our Daughters series stems from my organization's mission over the years of empowering teen girls across the country. On the next page, I would like to present the heartfelt letter I received from a special woman who will truly inspire you.

Dear Reader:

To teen girls who suffer from low self esteem, I would say that I have been there. We've all been there at some point in our lives, but the important thing to remember is that you are beautiful because you are full of life and a child of God. We are all beautiful and for every beauty, there is an eye to notice it. If you see the beauty in yourself, the world will follow suite so find something about yourself that you love.

Concerning skin color, as a dark-skinned girl I LOVE my color, but all my life people have been trying to convince me to hate it. But my opinion is the only one that matters, because it's my skin, my face and my body. Skin color does not determine the validity of your heart and beauty is so alive that it cannot be diminished by any stipulations such as skin color, a scar or weight. Beauty is so personal that it cannot be weighed against anyone else's. You are beautiful because you are. I wake up with myself every morning and I love ME. I wouldn't change myself for anything. Love yourself and all other opinions will fall to the wayside.

~ Actress GABOUREY SIDIBE (plays Precious in the film Precious -based on the novel Push by Sapphire)

ACT I

TO WHOM IT MAY CONCERN
Anonymous Letters

"Why do you tease me because of the color of my skin? You tease me because you don't understand the history of this brown velvet skin that carries the burden of my ancestors and the triumphs of our sisters that fought for our Civil Rights."

~Actress Nia Long

To Whom It May Concern:

This is to my parents of color.

The darkness in my soul has been overwhelming. You never gave me the light I needed to find my way. My existence was not a priority to you. Instead of giving me wings to soar, you clipped them. As your daughter, I needed your love, guidance, affection, and protection in order to build a strong foundation of self-worth, value, and respect. As a result of not receiving these things from both of you, I have suffered my whole life.

Facing the many consequences of my unwise choices has caused me a lot of pain, but I know it is necessary for my soul's healing and evolution. In order for me to peel back the many layers of my pain, I must explore the pain that prevented you both from pouring your love into my hungry soul.

Mama, I know that your birth was not a welcomed celebration, but a necessity. Being from the South, your parents' main reason for having children was to have them work in the cotton fields. Slavery was fresh in their minds and they carried the hidden pain and shame of that to all of you. They were not openly loving, affectionate or attentive, so they could not hear your silent cries of suffering until it was too late.

As the youngest girl with dark skin, you had a hard time accepting and loving yourself. You looked for it outside of yourself and soon found yourself trying to hide an unwanted pregnancy. You were prematurely considered a woman and had to drop out of high school. Back then it was a shameful disgrace for a young girl to have a baby out of wedlock. After the birth of your first child, you had to move away from home; you left your newborn daughter behind to be raised by your parents, in order to start a new life, but not having a strong sense of who you were made you weak and vulnerable.

Because you were still searching for love outside of yourself, you continuously attracted the wrong men into your life. Not knowing how to set high standards for yourself, you allowed undeserving men to use your precious body. You hungered for love, security, and a fairy-tale ending. The right man would rescue you and heal your hidden pain, but you didn't know how to sort out the lousy men.

Daddy, I also know that your birth was not a welcomed celebration. You were conceived as the result of your father's affair with a white woman. In 1927, it was considered a major violation for any black man to have sex with a white woman, let alone, to get her pregnant. For whatever reasons, you were carried to term. When you were extracted from her womb, you were immediately handed over to your father and forgotten by her. Your biological mother was happy to move on and forget about you. You were her secret shame. Your father took you home to his wife, and she accepted you as her own baby. You loved her deeply because she was a good mother to you.

However, that was interrupted when she died from breast cancer when you were fifteen. You begged God to save her, and when she died, you blamed Him for taking her away from you. You turned your back on God and, from that moment, your life became a living hell.

You were sent to live with your father's mother since he was not attentive to you, he was too busy chasing women and abusing alcohol. Your cousins, who lived there too, were cruel to you and teased you for being a mulatto. Your yellow complexion made them feel more uncomfortable with their darker hues. Stuck in the middle, you never felt you truly belonged. You hated white women because the one who abandoned you at birth hurt you to the core. You just wanted to be loved and thought that something was wrong with you when you didn't get it. You grew up fast and hard. Alcohol and women became a way for you to numb your pain.

Mama, when you met daddy, you were enamored by his handsome looks and light complexion. He was the answer to your unspoken prayers. You wanted security and believed you had found it with him. You couldn't see beyond your fantasy. In reality, he was unavailable. He was married with seven children and had even conceived another child with his wife's best friend.

He was a scavenger feeding [on] weak women like you. He was much older and wiser than you, so he played on your vulnerability and weakness. All of this knowledge still didn't prevent you from becoming pregnant by him, twice. You thought your life would become easier with all of the promises he fed you, but it didn't.

You learned the hard way, after you were stuck with two kids, that you had been bamboozled. You had allowed him to create a bigger mess of your life. I know it was a hard pill for you to swallow when he kept all of us hidden like a buried secret. His actions showed you that you were not special to him, and he had only used you for his own gratification. He never planned on leaving his wife for you, so he abandoned you with two kids that you were not prepared to take care of.

I often saw you crying because you were hurt and frustrated. You were his stand-by woman, and you accepted the little crumbs he tossed your way. You were willing to hold your breath, hoping he would change and come through on his many broken promises. He was a phantom man and father, spending time between two households. As a child, I never understood this. I didn't know why my daddy would show up at night and then disappear before morning.

Daddy, your ill treatment of mama also affected me. As the first man in my life, you were supposed to love me unconditionally; however, you taught me how to call the wolves to devour me. When you committed suicide, I felt stunned, confused and very angry at your final abandonment. The police took the note that you left me and never gave it back. For over sixteen years, I tried to guess what you said to me in that note. The curiosity nearly killed me. So forgive me for not being able to grieve your death; I had to begin the long journey of grieving my own life.

To all parents of color, I beg you to stop having children as proof that you can perform a sexual act. Children should be conceived as a result of a loving union, not as a consequence of unprotected sex. It is no benefit to the human race to have children that cannot be loved and enjoyed by both of their parents. If you cannot find love inside your own soul, you cannot afford to feed your child's soul.

Sincerely,

A Courageous Daughter

Dear Courageous Daughter:

Your pain is palatable. I could taste it, and the salt of your tears, as I read your letter. I'm so sorry you have suffered as much as you have. Every child needs to be loved. What is the toll on a child when he or she does not feel adored and special? The toll is immense, as you so eloquently discuss. As you say, wings can be clipped and deep pain can be experienced. And very often the toll is happening generation to generation, as was so in your case.

Parents who do not feel wanted and cherished often have children who also do not feel loved. You probably know that abuse can also be passed down through the generations. A parent who was beaten as a child is often guilty of beating his or her child. What a tragedy that pain in so many various forms can be transmitted from one generation to the next! You are very wise to be exploring your parents' pain as part of your healing process. Understanding why we have been short-changed from one generation to the next and seeing our parents as complex individuals, suffering with all sorts of pressures, both in the family and society, can really help us cleanse.

I hope your awareness of your own pain, combined with understanding the circumstances that influenced your parents' behaviors, is already helping you to cleanse. This seems to be the case, as you so poignantly ask your father's forgiveness for not grieving his death at the appropriate time.

Your plea to parents of color to stop having children as a result of unprotected sex, but rather because of a union of love, suggests that you are very determined to break the generational cycle. Though you still may yearn for love that you should have felt years ago, in a natural way, as the result of simply being a beloved child in a family, you have risen above those needs to take on a mission of correction.

I admire you and hope that you are in the process of cherishing your own soul, for many reasons, including the courage to speak out. I don't know if you have been in psychotherapy (the work you are doing is often part of the psychotherapeutic process). Whether you have or not, the type of insight you have and the strong convictions you have made, suggest that when you do have children you will nourish them fully and they will be a joy to you.

I wish you well.

Dr. Barbara Becker Holstein
Psychologist

"All I can say is you cannot change the color of your skin. Whether you are dark skinned or light skinned, love yourself, because self-love is more important than whether you are 'dark' or 'light' of skin."

~Singer/Actress Keke Palmer

To Whom It May Concern:

I have two beautiful daughters in high school. They both are doing great and they are loving individuals, but they are constantly at odds with each other over their skin color. One daughter has a lighter skin complexion than the other, and they are constantly using it to insult one another. Because of feelings of jealousy over perceptions about one being more attractive because of their shade of skin,

I hear arguments that escalate to name-calling. I have heard one [daughter] sling names [like] Darky, Spook, Shadow, and Oil Spot. Then I hear reactions like High Yellow, White Girl, and Light Bright, among others. I never thought my daughters would be faced with these stupid, spiteful, and meaningless name-calling problems because of their skin color.

I recently discovered that kids at the school actually have cliques dividing the light-skinned and dark-skinned blacks. My daughter even told me that the Caucasian girls of the school look at her as being white rather than black, and that is why she is being hated on by the darker skinned girls at the school. WHAT?!! I don't know what to tell them, because we never had this type of ludicrous behavior in my day by our black families. Why this type of behavior is being tolerated in our schools and community is beyond me.

We never had these issues of color when they were young, but these name-calling fights started as they entered middle school and have escalated with age. Their friend's preferences are obvious between them, [each] hanging out with one group of friends whose skin shade is close to their own. What's funny to me though is that they are more attracted to the opposite shade of color when it comes to dating. I have not figured that one out. It seems that the same thing occurs when we are adults. It makes no sense that sometimes we choose our partners based on the color of their skin.

I have always treated my daughters equally and for them to buy into this notion that one skin color is better than the other has me feeling helpless.

Sincerely,

A Father Looking For Clarity

Dear Father Looking For Clarity:

I imagine that the problem of your girls being at odds with each other about their skin problem is something you never dreamed would happen. When we raise kids we try to give them our best values and are shocked when they dwell on something that we never wasted time on.

In your case, it is their skin color. Believe me, there are hundreds of other dilemmas that also pop up in families. Sometimes there are two teenagers and one eats too much while the other is always dieting. Obviously in that case, even health issues can arise. In other families one child is good in sports while the other is a brain.

The result can be family members picking on the kid that is not good at sports and just the reverse, teasing the brain in the family. Sometimes there just doesn't seem to be a way to win as the parent.

The larger problem is a developmental one. Kids do need to find ways to distinguish themselves, both in the family and in school. One way or another, they will find a way to get attention. Much of that is normal behavior. However, since siblings are almost always competitive with one another, lots of times the ways they choose to get attention are at the cost of each other. That seems to be what is happening here.

I believe you are doing a good job. You should not be afraid to share with them your values and how you were brought up. Let them know that name-calling is always hurtful and doesn't benefit either party. Also, let them know what fairness is all about, and that it is their character traits and accomplishments that will ultimately create their destiny, not their skin tones.

Lastly, I would suggest that you disengage from some of this battle, as it is between them, not between you and the girls. In fact, you may be giving them so much attention around the issue that they will keep it going just to get attention.

Your best bet is to share your values and then to relax. Before you know it, they will probably be on to a new competitive issue between them. You need to rest a little so you will be ready for the next round!

Good luck.

Dr. Barbara Becker Holstein
Psychologist

Now I know you're under pressure

from work and the world

but please

watch how you hit me in front of our little girl.

She doesn't understand

this abuse her father feeds.

There's no believable excuse.

the truth, in my eyes she reads.

~ Actress/Queen of Spoken Word Georgia Me (excerpt from her
poem "Hit Like A Man")

To Whom It May Concern:

I just got off of the phone with my ex-wife. She called to let me know that my daughter is in the E.R. because a man put his hands on her. To say that I am angry is an understatement, because right now EVERY muscle in my body is twitching; my neck is stiffening and all I want to do is scream in rage. I want to find the fool that thought he could hurt my sweet child and not pay the consequence of my wrath. The only thing protecting him is the fact that I am 1,000 miles away and it's going to be a minute before I can get back to my baby girl.

As angry as I am, I am also confused by the fact that this is not the first time this boy had the nerve to disrespect my daughter. It's the first time my baby has been to the emergency room, but I have heard stories from people mentioning weird bruises or that she was isolating herself from family and friends. When I have voiced my concerns, she has always denied it or has given me some story to explain it away.

Being 1,000 miles away, I have always allowed myself to accept her stories and explanations. However, I know my daughter is a strong-willed and independent girl. She always has been, and even when I had to spank her, she always maintained her stubborn little ways. Even though it upset me as a parent, I certainly appreciated her sense of independence and willingness to stand by her convictions.

I just do not understand why she does not leave this fool. My daughter is a beautiful and intelligent woman. Even if she is still a young lady of nineteen, she is an old soul, wise beyond her age. I have heard and shared stories with her about friends she has counseled to get out of abusive relationships. This is why I am so shocked. How can she not see the forest through the trees? Why does she seem to deny what she is going through?

Lord, what have I done to fail my daughter? Did I make a mistake in putting my hands on her at such a young age? Was there a better way I could have handled it?

Lord, how do I amend my mistakes and help my daughter out of the abusive relationship she is in? What can I do to help her heal through this and break away from the destructive cycle?

Lord, as I prepare to make this journey to be with my child, I ask for your guidance, wisdom, and protection. I recognize that there is nothing you cannot resolve or mend. Lord, thank you for blessing me with such a beautiful daughter to cherish and protect. I also thank you for the continued guidance and love You bestow upon me.

In your name and the name of your son, Jesus Christ, amen.

Sincerely,

A Father Learning To Heal

Dear Father Learning To Heal:

First of all, it may be good news that your daughter is in the emergency room. Hopefully she is not seriously hurt. Assuming she is not, it is best that she is finally attended to by professionals. They may actually talk sense to her in a way that she can hear and maybe even direct her to some counseling services designed to help women leave abusive boyfriends and husbands.

She is not alone, as you may already realize. Many women are caught in the vicious cycle of staying with an abuser. She is young and that is on her side. Also she is not married and there are no children, at this time. All of that makes exiting easier.

I do think both you and your ex-wife can be very helpful at this time. Perhaps it is a blessing that you live 1,000 miles away. It would be ideal if your daughter could come and live [near] you for a while. That would be the easiest way for her to break ties with this fellow. I don't know what she does, but perhaps she can attend college near you or get a job.

I think visiting her at this time and offering to help her move away from the situation, in a loving manner, would be a great step. Your ex-wife can hopefully work with you in encouraging her to separate from the fellow. Even if she stays living where she currently resides, your ex-wife can help her obtain counseling. That is really critical now, so she can understand, from a trained therapist, the nature of abusive relationships. By the way, even if she comes to live near you, make sure that she gets into some counseling or a support group for women who have been abused.

As far as what you did when she grew up, spanking, although

not at all encouraged in today's world, was a traditional way of punishing for many years. In most cases, it did not damage the child, although psychologists and educators have determined that there are better methods to teach positive behaviors to kids. Of course, there is a big difference between a spanking and a beating. I'm taking you at your word.

If you have been a loving parent, but used spanking as a disciplinary method, I don't think you need to beat yourself up. Rather, understand that it is possible your daughter has some resentment for the spankings and maybe some feelings surrounding that form of punishment. Just talk to her about it. It will only bring the two of you closer to share your concerns, and above all, give her your time, your wisdom, your love, and your helpfulness. You can do it! Your love is coming through in the letter. Now, go to her.

All my best,

Dr. Barbara Becker Holstein
Psychologist

"Speak into her life until you see her blossom into the strong, intelligent, empowered woman she was destined to become."

~ Actress/Entrepreneur Lisa Wu Hartwell

To Whom It May Concern:

I always thought this type of tragedy only occurred in the movies. I never in my wildest imagination or fears thought this life-changing event would happen to me. I suffered the horror of watching my wife of ten years die while giving birth to our daughter.

When we arrived at the hospital it was supposed to be one of the happiest days of my life, yet I was rudely awakened when my wife complained to the doctor of not feeling [well] and suddenly she was gone. The doctors moved quickly to try and revive my wife, but they also worked to rescue our little baby girl.

Where do I begin sharing my true feelings about this life-changing ordeal my family and I went through? I wondered when and how I would tell my little girl about her mother, and what happened on the day she was born. I struggled with figuring out how I would tell our other children that their mother was not coming home. How would I continue on? These and so many other questions flooded my mind.

The day finally came when my little girl was able to come home from the hospital with me. I thought about how much she looked like her mother, from her eyes, nose, and all the way down to her little toes.

In years past, I had always been able to stay busy around the house, at my job, and I never took life for granted. I certainly was not going to start then, and I thank God for the previous training my parents instilled in me and my siblings for cooking and cleaning.

During that first month, I spent countless hours holding my little girl and didn't let her out of my sight. I began asking myself every day, "Why me GOD?" As I asked for his blessings and guidance to get me through those days and nights, spent thinking and dreaming about my wife, I knew that life is a test where we will be challenged with ups and downs while on this earth.

My whole family, especially my mother and mother-in-law have supported me through this experience. I remember waking up alone in my bed and feeling the sunrays peeking through the blinds. The rays shone on my dresser onto a picture that my ten-year-old niece drew for me.

The picture had words of encouragement about faith and God. It was exactly what I needed at that moment. The love that I have experienced has allowed me to grow stronger as a man and father to my children.

I have always been a great father and provider for all of my children and have always been there for them, but there will be a special bond with my new daughter that will never be broken. I look forward to my daughter getting older so I can share with her how wonderful her mother was and just how much she loved her. I pray that she will grow to become the same kind of inspirational woman that her mother was.

Sincerely,

A Father Remembering His Loving Wife & Loving His Newborn Daughter

Dear Father Remembering His Loving Wife & Loving His Newborn Daughter:

I am so impressed with your resilience and the deep devotion to both your wife and new baby girl. Of course it is a tragedy to lose a spouse in such a heartbreaking way and watching a treasured life leave as a new life begins. Yet, your handling of the loss speaks volumes to your strong character and your determination to make the world safe and loving for your family.

Your first concerns are for your new baby and for her siblings. You are right where you should be. I don't know exactly what you said to your children when the baby came home, but I am sure you reassured them that they would always be loved and cared for. Also, you have welcomed the support that your family has given you, including your mother and your mother-in-law.

This is great. The kids will pick up on this and see that you are permitting others who love them to stay fully in their lives. This is important. Not only will you really need their help, but [also] it gives the children permission to share their feelings and time with other loving family members. Kids need what grandparents can offer in terms of unconditional love and the sense of continuity of belonging to a generational family.

Also I am sure the children pick up on your faith. This is also critical. They too need faith and to believe that their mom is safe and still [a] part of them. I would encourage you to share with them your beliefs, when the timing is appropriate. Wait for their lead. Let them ask questions and then be there to guide them. Meanwhile, certainly share with them that you know their mother is safe and still loves them deeply.

I know you will help your little girl bond deeply to your wife's memory as she grows. However, don't leave the other children out. They also need to feel special and just as important to their mother as the baby and to feel that she loved them with her total heart also. Let everyone share in her radiance!

May you be healed in your own pain and have the pleasure of raising fine children, and children who have your strengths, and depth, and their mother's inspirational characteristics!

Lastly, you seem very strong, but I will just mention that if you need it, many hospitals offer grief-counseling groups. Often in these groups there will be a diversity of people, from those who have lost a spouse after sixty years to those who have lost a child. The leader, a trained mental health counselor, leads the group through many aspects of the grief process. These are usually time-limited groups. All of my patients who have attended such groups have praised them tremendously.

All my best,

Dr. Barbara Holstein
Psychologist

"Each person should feel the pride of God's creation and we should each make the 'finished product' a work of art and productivity."

~ Civil Rights Activist\Founder of Trumpet Awards Xernona Clayton

To Whom It May Concern:

Where should I begin about the life changing issues I faced in raising my brother's daughter? First of all, I never asked to be in that position. I was merely her uncle and had been divorced for more than a year when she came into my life. When my brother died, [in his will] I was named the sole guardian of his seven-year-old daughter.

It was a responsibility that definitely forced me to change the ways of my single lifestyle. There could not be any more running the streets and being out all hours of the night on weekends, and of course I certainly could not indulge my favorite craving, women. This was one of the hardest changes, considering that I was accustomed to having them available throughout the week.

Clearly, now, having her in my life forced me to re-direct my views and actions about the way I should treat women. It took time to get used to having a young girl around the house. Over the years we both built up the trust to engage in great conversations about school, friends, and questions she had about growing up.

After eight years together, the young lady turned fifteen and was in the ninth grade. Her daily routine was to come home with constant questions about boys. Could she ask me anything else?!? I decided that I should sit down and teach her how boys should treat her and her girlfriends, as the queens they are.

I sat her down and wrote up my three pet peeves for her, concerning boys.

> 1st - Boys should always be gentlemen to her and never raise their voice and/or say angry comments to her, even if they are mad.

2nd - Boys should open doors for her and always let her go into a room first (of course, she really liked that one).

3rd - UNDER NO CIRCUMSTANCES should a boy ever hit a girl or threaten to hurt her.

Those were my three pet peeves that I tried to instill in my niece. She was a young lady that I considered my own loving daughter, and I truly loved and wanted to protect her.

At twenty-six she is now happily married to a young man who is a great husband. He treats her like a queen, and I can honestly say that I see that I had a positive impact on how she viewed her relationships with men.

As fathers or uncles or males in any little girl's life, we, as men, have an obligation to take the time to teach our girls how they should be treated by people, and males, in particular. We must show them the warning signs of unhealthy relationships, and support them when and if they find
themselves in danger of one.

When I came into this relationship years ago, I felt like I was going to be a babysitter for my niece, but through it all, she actually taught me how to be a father.

Sincerely,

A Man Learning to Become a Positive Father

Dear Positive Father:

You have succeeded! You are indeed a Positive Father. I am very impressed with the ways that you have brought up your niece, particularly as you never expected to take her father's place. It is fascinating how your life was changed by your niece. The responsibilities seemed to take hold of you instantly and you quickly changed your lifestyle.

Many people cannot change as appropriately and quickly as you did. Children who have distressing social, emotional, and academic problems can be the result of the neglect that comes from adults living a lifestyle that does not go with raising a kid. Good for you that you came up to the plate so quickly!

I am very impressed with the way your relationship developed as your niece grew into her teens. She appears to have trusted you with her emotional and social needs. That's wonderful, and you responded by always listening to her and answering her questions.

How simple, yet so many parents just don't listen to their kids! You can't imagine how many parents walk away just when a child is trying to finally express something or who just appear to be listening when a child is asking an important question, but are really counting calories or doing a grocery list in their heads.

You not only listened, but you gave on-target learning lessons that were really helpful to her. Rather than trying to divert her interests away from boys (which I believe would not have worked anyway) you helped her build a sense of pride about herself while learning how to evaluate the young men that came into her life. You were psychologically right on. She ended up being able to recognize unhealthy traits in a young man, but also feel special about herself. That was a win-win for both of you.

And the proof of the pudding is that, at twenty-six, she is married to a great young man who treats her like a queen.

Sounds to me like you raised a great daughter and, of course, that does make you one great dad. I think you will be a great grandpa also.

Dr. Barbara Becker Holstein
Psychologist

"Don't pay attention to anyone who is living in the past and color struck!"

~ Mother Love

To Whom It May Concern:

Growing up as a young white boy I was never truly aware of what racial prejudice was. Both of my parents raised me to see people as God's children. I was brought up learning that the color of a person's skin was irrelevant because our souls were transparent and that God loves all of us the same.

The first encounter I had with racism came when I was 4, and I was at lunch with my grandmother's best friend. I was an outgoing and friendly little boy having a meal with a wonderful black woman who loved me as if I were her own grandchild.

As we were preparing to leave, a man and his son came in, and Jean offered them the table that we were vacating. The man made a face and muttered something under his breath as he walked past us. Jean just shook her head sadly and called him a big goat and then we left the restaurant to get ice cream cones at our favorite place.

It was years later that I discovered she had called the man a bigot and that his disrespect was because of the color of her skin. That was a moment that helped to shape the man I grew up to be. It has also been a factor in the father that I strive to be for my daughter.

In fact, I have always been pleased that my daughter is color blind in the same way that her parents are. We have raised her in a loving home and taught her by example the love she should have for all of her fellow humans.

Little did I know that her first real experience with racism would come from two people that she loved and trusted with all her heart. You see, I married a black woman from a southern state, and I was unaware of the prejudices she overcame growing up. It seems that both of her parents are racists, but they have never been blatant about it. In all of the time that I have been with my wife, I had never witnessed anything that would make me aware of their feelings towards Caucasians.

It was not until my daughter was a teenager and brought her first white boyfriend, Jeremy, with us to a family reunion that I witnessed their racism. Jeremy and my daughter have been best friends since they were in grade school, so my wife and I were not surprised when love blossomed between them. In fact, we got along wonderfully with his parents and had even taken vacations together. That is why we invited Jeremy to come along with us that fateful weekend.

The four-hour car ride was spent talking about football, politics, and which colleges the kids were considering. When we arrived at the park, we could see several generations of extended family setting up food, drinking cold beverages, and starting pick-up games of football and basketball. The atmosphere was filled with love and laughter. Of course, that is before my in-laws betrayed my daughter's trust and love.

It was subtle at first. They kept stealing looks at Jeremy as he played basketball with my daughter's cousins. Then I thought I overheard a slur slip from her grandfather, but it was said so quickly that I was sure that I had misheard him. Nobody else reacted to it, so I let it slide. Later I heard my mother-in-law say something about mixing bloodlines and I was shocked. I found my wife and shared my concerns with her. She said that she was embarrassed about it, but it was something that she was used to hearing and that they grew up in a different time and did not mean anything by it.

I was angry and concerned, but I chose to keep it in check. I did not want my daughter to see my emotions and question what was going on. I hoped that she had not heard or seen the things that her elders were saying and doing. For most of the day, they seemed to behave around her, but then my father-in-law showed my daughter his true colors when he asked her why she was dating someone outside of her own race.

In that moment, I do not know what made me angrier, the hateful words used about a young man that I loved like my own son or the devastating look of pain and betrayal on my baby girl's face. As I saw the tears well up in my daughter's eyes, it was all that I could do not to punch my father-in-law square in the mouth.

She jumped from the table and ran off before the tears fell. My wife and Jeremy both ran after her. All I could do was stare and shake, as I contemplated why I should not physically harm the man who hurt my daughter. My father-in-law just stared back at me and smirked. Right at that moment, it took every ounce of self-control for me to turn my back and go find my daughter. Everyone around the table was completely silent, with no one making a move. I simply walked off and never looked back.

When I reached my daughter, I took her into my arms and just let her shake with the tears that fell freely. Jeremy would not look me or my wife in the eye, and I cannot say that I blamed him. It was a long and silent trip home. I did notice that there was an uncomfortable space between Jeremy and my daughter, which seemed to get wider as the ride went on.

After dropping Jeremy off at the house, my daughter began to cry again in the backseat. She knew that racism existed and said she had certainly dealt with it from strangers, but she could not understand why her grandfather would say such a hateful thing to her. I had no idea how to respond to her, because I wasn't sure what to say myself.

I was angry and trying very hard not to let it show or seem as if it was directed at her or Jeremy. Even though my wife was aware of how her father is, she also had no idea how to console our daughter. For now the question has just remained unanswered.

It has been a few weeks since all of this unfolded, and we have not seen Jeremy at the house at all. My daughter says that they are still dating, but he is not sure how to act or speak around us. I have not been sure how to handle it myself, so I have not talked with either of his parents yet.

I know that my daughter and her boyfriend are hurting, and Lord that is why I am asking You for guidance.

Lord, I do not understand why there are people who allow prejudice to exist because of a person's skin color. Lord, I continue to try and live a humble and obedient life, but right now, I am having a difficult time with the anger I feel towards the man who hurt my daughter. Lord, how do I help my daughter to heal from the mental wounds inflicted upon her?

Lord, I know that there is nothing that You cannot heal or mend, and now I am beseeching You to help my family to heal. I am also asking that You bind the spirits of contempt and hatred that fuel the energy it takes to feel prejudice against others.

I thank you Lord for hearing me and accepting my prayers. Amen.

Sincerely,

A Father Looking For Help

Dear Father Looking For Help:

Racial and also religious prejudices are always hurtful and often dangerous. I'm sorry you encountered racial prejudice right in the midst of your own extended family. I have a suggestion for you. I have to assume that you, your wife, and daughter have been involved with your wife's family over many years. I also have to assume that they love their daughter, their granddaughter, and care for you.

Given those assumptions, I would say that walking away from them would be a mistake. We all need our families. Perhaps it is time to go and visit and have a sincere discussion with them. They may need to be reminded that their granddaughter is already of mixed blood. This does not change the person she is or their rights and privileges to love and be with her. However, she will fall in love and marry whomever is right for her, whatever his bloodlines. Whether their skin tones match is not relevant. What is relevant is how they treat each other and the life they can make together.

If your in-laws can respect that, then they are welcome to share and be a part of your daughter's future. If they have trouble with this, then they may indeed find themselves locked out of many joyous events.

It may also make sense to have Jeremy over to your home to let him know your feelings about him and what you have chosen to make clear to your wife's parents. Of course, another possibility, if face-to-face is too painful, is to put the concepts outlined above in a letter to your wife's parents.

You mention feeling a lot of anger toward your wife's father. That may be one reason to write rather than visit, as displaying anger will not help this situation. He is, as all of us are, of his time and place in the history of mankind. Coming at him in anger, rather than in calm dialogue and realistic insight, will not help him, you, your wife or your daughter.

Whatever you choose, as you and your wife clarify your positions to everyone involved, hopefully the air will be cleared and your daughter and Jeremy can be comfortable with each other again. Just one more caveat, sometimes relationships just fall apart anyway at your daughter's age. If that happens, I am sure another fine young man will enter her life. Still, the work you and your wife do now to clear the air with family can only help.

Good luck!

Dr. Barbara Becker Holstein
Psychologist

"You are the young queens of this Earth! You are the future wives, mothers and nurturers of our culture and people."

~Grammy Artist/Actress Jill Scott

To Whom It May Concern:

Today is both a joyful and sad day for me. In just a few hours, I will be walking my only daughter down the wedding aisle. As I hear her mother, aunts, and girlfriends all bustling around the house getting ready, I flashback to earlier times in my daughter's young life.

I think back to a time before she was even interested in boys. Life was simpler then, because she loved *Sesame Street*, roller-skating, and tea parties with her stuffed animals. When she had slumber parties, there was no talk of boys. Instead they would listen to music, watch scary movies, snack on junk food, and play games.

Then my baby became a teenager, and she and her friends began to pay more attention to boys. I have always been so proud of her ability to maintain focus through that period of time. She always expected and received the respect she gave and deserved. Even when she dated a few boys that I found questionable, my daughter always recognized the difference between love and hormone-driven physical desires.

As my little girl transitioned into a young woman in college, I was so proud of her continued accomplishments. When she brought home a young man during fall break of her junior year, I was certainly guarded about liking or disliking him. I had to be, because I had already heard so many stories of other daughters losing their focus when a boyfriend entered the picture.

As that long weekend passed, I began to recognize that this young man was a strong complement to my daughter. He was respectful to all of us, and he proved to be intelligent and ambitious.

I was proud to hear that he was maintaining a 4.0 G.P.A. in school, and he had already been accepted to a graduate school on an academic scholarship. Even more important to me, this young man was supportive of my daughter's success. It seems they had been friends since high school, but they had not started dating until that year when they realized they were falling in love.

It was at the end of that weekend that they asked for my blessing, but they also reassured me it would be a long engagement since they both wanted to finish their undergraduate degrees first. I discussed it with her mother, my own wife of twenty-three years, and we both agreed that it was definitely a union worth blessing.

So now, here I am preparing to allow another man to become my daughter's primary protection on Earth. I suddenly realize how my wife's father felt twenty-three years ago, or how my mother's father felt fifty years ago, as they traveled down this same emotional path.

Lord, thank you for the blessings. Not just today or yesterday, but all the days that you have created. Thank you Lord, for being the rock and the shield during the tough times we have had. Thank you for your love and for the wisdom You have imparted to us all. I thank you again Lord, for the wonderful times and for blessing my family with such a beautiful daughter.

Lord, we also thank you for bringing together our daughter with this wonderful man. We thank you for allowing them to sow the seeds of friendship before becoming caught up in an intimate relationship. Again Lord, we thank you for the continued blessings that You provide us all with. Amen.

Now I must move on and prepare to transport everybody to the church. Thank you for allowing me to share this.

Sincerely,

Father Of The Bride

Dear Father Of The Bride:

You have done a wonderful job raising your daughter and may only good news come to you as she and her husband start their life's journey together. I am so impressed with how you have brought up your daughter. It is clear that you have always been respectful of her and of each developmental stage she has gone through.

You seem to have appreciated each stage, from tea parties, to slumber parties, to college days. Although it seems you are experiencing some sense of loss, as she is about to marry, "this wonderful young man," you also realize that this is the nature of life. With wisdom you now realize how your father-in-law felt.

I like the way you got to know your future son-in-law and did not pre-judge him. Also, I admire how you discussed everything with your wife and gave your blessing jointly to them. Lastly, your devotion to the Almighty and your capacity for gratitude shine through this letter.

Prayerful people are often happier and more grateful than those who don't pray. Simply put, I think you are doing everything right!

All my best,

Dr. Barbara Becker Holstein
Psychologist

"Everything in life starts and ends with GOD the ALMIGHTY and if you have and know GOD in your heart you know that he/she does not make mistakes!"

~Oscar Nominated Actress Taraji P. Henson

To Whom It May Concern:

I received a voicemail about a half hour ago from my son-in-law. It seems that he and my daughter got into an argument. He walked out of the house before his temper got the better of him. He has asked if I could meet him to talk because he is concerned over the anger that he still feels. To make it worse, he said that he came very close to hitting hit her tonight, which is also why he has left for the night.

I am struggling with mixed emotions right now. On one hand, I am glad that he had the sense to leave before making a mistake, but given his abusive upbringing, I understand the risk of him not avoiding it the next time. This is a young man that I love as if he were my own son, so I certainly want to help him however I can right now.

When my baby brought this young man home, I liked him, but I sensed a hard edge about him that concerned me. It was not until I got to know him better, and we began to bond as men, that he shared his past with me. I discovered that his father was an angry man who had raised him in a strict, aggressive, and abusive way. My son-in-law shocked me with stories of being slammed into walls, kicked across the room, belittled for perceived failures, and made to feel like less of a man if he EVER showed any signs of emotion or sensitivity. It made me understand the edge that I sensed when I first met this young man.

I never really saw him lose his temper, but I had witnessed him get tense when things seemed to irritate him. When I had talked to my daughter about it, she always reassured me that he had never threatened her or spoken disrespectfully. She said that she had seen him get angry before, but that he had never become aggressive from it. In fact, the only time she or I had seen him be aggressive was in his wrestling tournaments or mixed martial arts competitions.

After I heard about his abusive past, I thought that he had discovered a healthy outlet for his anger by participating in athletics. He was a two-time All-State strong safety in high school football. As a junior wrestler, he placed second in State in the 145-pound class and the next year he was a State Champion in the 160-pound class. He was offered scholarships for his athletic talents in both wrestling and football, but he was also offered a full-ride scholarship for his intellect.

He chose to go with brain instead of brawn, and accepted the academic scholarship. It was during his sophomore year that he met my daughter and eventually the rest of her family. A week before his graduation, he asked for my permission to marry my daughter. I must admit that I had some minor concerns about his past, but in the year-and-a-half that I watched him continue to grow and mature as a man, I buried those concerns and gave him my blessing. The night before his commencement, he popped the question and my daughter accepted through tears of joy. They took a year to plan the wedding, and have been married for six years now.

As a man, husband, and father, I understand that men and women have arguments and that communication can get crossed up. Right now, I have to figure out how and what I need to say to my son (yes, I consider him my son), to help him. He certainly knows that a problem is on the horizon if we do not break the cycle of domestic violence right now.

Lord, I am turning to You for guidance, because I know that there is NOTHING that You cannot handle. I recognize that I also need your help in teaching my son to learn how to become the man You expect us to be. I was fortunate enough when You guided me to the men's group at church all those years ago, and now I am moved to establish that for our current congregation.

Lord, please guide my words and actions as I prepare to meet with my son. I know that this is a major obstacle for him and for my daughter. I know that this is an opportunity for Satan to attack both my son and myself, so as I prepare to leave and meet up with him, I lift my boy up to You. Just as You gave us your only Son, I am prepared to do whatever is necessary to help guide my son in your word.

Lord, You have told us that as men we must take responsibility and not be passive. This is a mighty wound in my son's soul, and it is your love and the blood of your own Son that will begin to heal that wound and pain.

Lord, I thank you for all of the blessings that You continue to grace our lives with. I thank you for the love that You continue to bestow upon us. I thank you for your guidance and the opportunities for continued growth.

Lord, as I take my keys and prepare to drive out to meet my son, I thank you for the armor You provide me with and the angels that surround us all every day. Lord, in your name and the name of your Son, Jesus Christ, I thank you. Amen.

Sincerely,

A Father Continuing To Learn And Teach About Being the Man God Expects

Dear Father Continuing To Learn And Teach About Being the Man God Expects:

It is very clear that you are a man of deep faith and wisdom. You understand fully the risks involved for your son in the upbringing he has had. You also understand the risk for your own emotions and perhaps actions to get out of comfort's range when you meet him. You have asked the Lord for guidance and advice.

I am only a psychologist, but my advice is simple and to the point. I would resist meeting with him face-to-face, at this time. That is for both of your sakes. Rather, I would suggest calling him on the phone and honestly voicing not only your love for him, but also your concerns. The best thing for him now is professional guidance, not a meeting with you that you might both regret.

I would encourage him to join a group that specializes in anger management. He can find one through the local hospitals or mental health organizations. It would also be wonderful for him to work one-on-one with a counselor who specializes in abusive behavior patterns.

If money is an issue, helping him financially to obtain the help he needs should benefit the daughter you love, as well as him. The faster he gets help, the better. The next time he may not be able to keep his hands at his sides! I hope you can reach him quickly and help him to get the guidance he needs.

Dr. Barbara Becker Holstein
Psychologist

"There's no way any one of us can be beautiful to all people. When I find things to appreciate about myself I feel more beautiful."

~ Actress Sanaa Lathan

To Whom It May Concern:

Pledge Master, I forgive you for imprisoning me for forty-two years.

On December 23, 2008, I took a trip to New Orleans, Louisiana. While there, I took a bus tour through the wards devastated most by Hurricane Katrina. Shortly after boarding the bus, my mind regressed back to my first visit to New Orleans. I was a lowly pledge to your fraternity and you provided me the opportunity to go to a graduate-level smoker-party.

Suddenly the tour guide pulled me from my stream of consciousness with an announcement over the P.A. system. We had arrived at the first walking-tour where the levy had broke and killed so many, and it was time to de-board. Shivering to the bone, I stepped down from the front of the tour bus on that misty, cold, and windy afternoon. As I gawked at the physical and human devastation, and void left by Katrina, my mind again drifted back to that darker day nearly forty-two years ago.

We were a group of Phi Beta Sigma Fraternity pledges taking a road trip from Baltimore City, Maryland to a smoker-party in Grambling, Louisiana. Though we had no idea what to expect from the made-Greeks hosting the party, we were anxious, excited, and grateful to be chosen.

On the way to Grambling, we stopped for a side-trip to New Orleans to visit the infamous Bourbon Street. Tucked away in the French Quarter, Bourbon Street is part of a city that I love to describe as that chic city of jazz and seafood, chilling below the Mississippi River.

It was in this epic metropolis of canals, viaducts, levies, and swamps, where two distinctly different cultures continue to co-exist, that I found that Bourbon Street continues to be what I remembered. It is a melting pot of jazz-loving, partying strangers from all over the world. Black, white, yellow or whatever, skin color seems not to matter. As a young man, I was afraid of the South, but Bourbon Street was a friendly neon light in a wilderness of hatred and fear for a young black male visiting the Delta Region for the first time.

I was anxious to get to the party and saw it as a place where I could feel comfortable and safe among my own kind. Nothing could have been further from the truth. As I got closer to the fraternity house, I noticed a bottleneck forming at the front porch's stairwell entrance. It seemed that certain people were being turned away.

As we got to the porch landing, I found myself in front of a big, fat, freckle-faced, high-yellow bouncer who refused me entrance. When I protested, because I felt entitled to enter, he said, "Don't you understand the rule?"

"What rule?" I retorted. "I don't know what you're talking about. I'm not from here. I'm from Baltimore, Maryland."

"I don't give a damn where you're from," he said. "You didn't pass the brown-paper-bag test, nigger."

"What brown-paper-bag test?" I asked, as I proceeded to press by him.

Pointing up, he yelled, "The brown-paper-bag hanging above your head, nigger," while at the same time pushing me down the steps.

In those days, calling a black man or woman a nigger was a

declaration of war. I was seriously pissed off and ready to fight. Looking up in shock and anger, as I picked myself up from the ground, I said, "Yes, I see the bag, but, why did you have to push me?"

"I pushed you because I wanted to, you f—king black-ass mother-f—king nigger," he shouted and simultaneously picked up a trashcan, and threw it at me.

As I hit the ground again, I heard him screaming, "Anyone darker than that brown-paper-bag, as you are, is not welcome in this house."

Picking myself up again, I made for the steps, but found myself dragged away by light-skinned associate pledges. It was disarmingly humiliating for me to be verbally demeaned and physically attacked by people I considered to be my kind. I still have a crystal clear image of the huge group of mulattos who had gathered on the porch, from the party, who were pointing and laughing at what had happened to me.

For so many years I have resented you, and in those early years my resentment bordered on hate. It was that air of superiority and swagger you had because you knew that your high-yellow skin and straight hair afforded you social options and opportunities that your darker skinned counterparts, like me, would never be offered or find access to.

I resented you when you always got the prettiest and smartest females. I resented you when you got A's and B's in college classes that you seldom showed up for. I resented you, because with no talent, you fit the preferred demographic profile and got a TV anchor job.

I resented you because you got to be the model; you got to be the film star; you got to be the lead; you got to be the banker, the lawyer, the doctor, the teacher; you got to be the host; you got to be the president. I'm sure by now you get my point. I resented you because you made me feel helpless and sometimes valueless, knowing that no matter what I did I would never be high yellow, with straight hair.

I resented you most because I believed you knew what would happen to me when you sent me to that University Greek smoker-party. You were the local leader of an international brotherhood organization that predicated the foundation of its existence on service to the disenfranchised, honor, integrity, and discipline. However, that experience heightened my distrust and resentment for light-skinned blacks, broke my heart, made me suspect of black people in roles of leadership, and worse it made me question the meaning of the word brotherhood.

You robbed me of my dignity, but worse than that, you robbed me of my illusions of self-worth and brotherly protection. You shattered my self-esteem. I had to get it back, and get it back I did.

I dated upscale, financially independent, drop-dead gorgeous white women for twenty years. Within that period, I married a Jewish princess lawyer. I know now that those women were really playing field levelers and trophies for me. They said to the world that I was of value because dark-skinned me was able to capture what most black men, light- or dark-skinned, could never catch. I got the coveted, well-educated cosmopolitan white woman. Black men, mostly light-skinned, would often ask, "How did you get that woman?"

I would smile and say nothing. During those twenty years, skin color was not a conscious issue for me, but it was still there eating away at my psyche, like a swarm of termites. The brown-paper-bag test was a serious epiphany for me. It took me back to high school, where, despite my high academic class standing, I was not encouraged to go on to college. I did not fit the pedigree of light, bright, and almost white.

It was then that I began to notice that practically all of the educators, professionals, business owners, performers, entertainers, and anybody who was anybody, in what was then referred to as the black ghetto, was a mulatto or a light-skinned person.

I got to go to college because I challenged the practice of refusing academic scholarships to academically qualified dark-skinned students. I refused to go away, and thank God I had back-up. My backup was my revered, but often feared, grandfather.

My grandfather was black as tar. He had a green-eyed, high-yellow wife and five light-skinned children. A doctor of theology and the Presiding Elder to the North Carolina Conference of African Episcopal Methodist Churches, he aggressively spoke up for me and placed his reputation on the line.

More importantly, my grandfather was the Pastor of Bethel AME Church, which at that time was the most elite AME church in Baltimore's colored community. Though a sometimes petrifying, fire and brimstone preacher, the love and respect for my grandfather and his family far extended the Baltimore metropolitan community. Thanks to my grandfather's faithful community activism along with the fierce guidance and strong support of my single, head-of-household mother, my two sisters and I graduated from college.

My college experience not only solidified my goal of finishing college, it also added a desire to seek higher degrees, which I did. College took me education, enhanced housing, and upgraded white-collar employment.

When I was a graduate student studying communication science, I coined the term "Skitzomelaninocracy" to describe the phenomenon of lighter-skinned people discriminating against darker hued individuals within the same ethnic group. "Skitzomelaninocracy" reared its ugly head during slavery. White slave owners saw all blacks as inferior and sub-human people.

Lighter complexioned blacks, often rejected by their sperm-donor slave-masters, were assigned less labor-intensive indoor work, while the darker-skinned slaves were generally relegated to hard and arduous outdoor labor. Light-skinned blacks were often given freedmen papers, houses, businesses, large parcels of land, were allowed to travel between states, and gain entry to Ivy-League and prestigious colleges and universities.

The brown-paper-bag test was a traditional and demeaning ritual utilized by Negro and Creole fraternities and sororities to discriminate against anyone they decided was too dark. These sororities and fraternities locked-out anyone whose skin was darker than a paper lunch bag.

It is also believed that the brown-paper-bag test had been used in the application screening process at prestigious historically black colleges. The [schools] would require potential students to submit photographs, to ensure that the majority of the student-body would be of lighter complexions.

Skin color and the unpredictable ways that different people react to it has been a paradox of gargantuan proportion to me since I was a seven-year-old, when I demanded that my mother let me drink from the public water-fountain labeled "White Only" or explain to me why I couldn't.

I had no clue why she began to cry. She didn't answer my question. I was in college when I suddenly understood the reason for her silence and the pain I must have caused her when she had no words to help me. She was the red-bone mother of a darker-skinned black male child.

Since I was seven years old, I have wrestled with the question, "What does it mean for me to be black in America?"

At age 64, I went to Brazil. It was while I was in Brazil that I finally mended the broken heart created in Louisiana. Maybe it was that their socio-psychological freedom was so implicit in their nude beaches. Maybe it was the huge African presence and their full integration into the socio-economic fabric of the Brazilian culture. Maybe it was the fact that they distrusted Caucasians, but embraced me, or maybe it was because they worked so hard to help me work through the language barrier.

Whatever it was, it opened my mind and helped me to see that until I forgave that line-chief, who was so brutal in his fragmenting of my ego, I would never know true peace. So I forgave him, and at that very moment, my life changed for the better. I saw clearer. I began taking risks, and I started dreaming of entrepreneurial endeavors again. Moreover, I actually started to chase my dreams. I acquired a new home, and I gave myself permission to invite a new woman into my life.

I began to understand that I had let the brown-paper-bag test help me build a network of negatively charged bars around my psyche, relative to my skin color, and that it had in some fashion shaped every life decision I ever made.

Mr. Pledge Master, your tape was always in my head, even when I was not conscious of it, you were always there whispering and taunting, "You're a dark-skinned man in America." I allowed it to turn me back into that little seven-year-old boy who couldn't even get a drink at the public park's water fountain.

No one wanted to drink behind him because he had dark-skin and nappy hair. Again and again, I became that seven-year-old boy who so many times heard himself referred to by family, and so called friends, neighbors and strangers as black-nigger, dumb, dirty, nappy-headed monkey, ape, ashy-black, ugly, ink-spot, worthless, one who would never amount to anything, and other obscenities that I choose not to repeat.

So I am writing this letter to you to say that I forgive you.

May God bless and keep you in His light.

Sincerely yours,

A Man Who Has Overcome The Brown Paper Bag Test

Dear Man Who Has Overcome The Brown Paper Bag Test:

First of all, let me congratulate you on your wonderful capacities of resiliency and courage. As a psychologist, I am always impressed by the emotional and spiritual powers of some people to overcome adversity. I am sorry to say, that not all of us have such an inner force to draw upon. It is obvious that you do have that force, and you have also realized that forgiveness is usually a final step in letting go of demoralizing pain that we carry within ourselves.

There are many people unable to draw from their personal well of strength. They have been too broken by life's challenges and hurts. For some there is no return if the ego is shattered once too often by cruel remarks or deeds.

As people, this is why we need to understand how vicious prejudice really is. It is not only the remarks and attitudes of the people outside of ourselves. No, it is much more. It is the way we absorb prejudice and turn against ourselves or our own people. Once this happens, the 'others' who have worked so hard to put us down or take privileges away from us don't even have to work that hard anymore. We are doing lots of the work for them.

I am especially proud to become the responding psychologist starting with this volume of the Saving Our Daughters book series, because the color of our skin is a critical issue. It breaks my heart as a psychologist to see a man or a woman, boy or girl, stifled or emotionally crushed by a reaction to their skin tone.

Not only have these types of reactions, such as what you experienced, led to cruelty and death, be it a literal physical death or the emotional death of a human being with lots of potential, but this type of prejudice is a universal metaphor for all people. How many millions have died for having a different religion, keeping a different culture, or having different physical characteristics? Too many to count.

Thank you for sharing so intimately your trials and tribulations. You are a role model for all of us. May we all have the strength to forgive and be true to our unique beings. Even more so, may we have the courage to give up artificial barriers and hatreds between each other and ourselves!

May your life be filled with peace and harmony.

Dr. Barbara Becker Holstein
Psychologist

ACT II

TO WHOM IT MAY CONCERN
Letters From A Man's Point Of View

"I believe people today are more attracted to physical appearance and social/career status rather than skin color."

~ Idris Elba

Our first father, Idris Elba, is a tremendous actor. He has starred opposite Beyonce Knowles in the film *Obsessed* and in the hit comedy *The Office*. Elba is perhaps best known for his role as Stringer Bell in the acclaimed HBO drama *The Wire*, and has starred with Denzel Washington in the big-screen success, *American Gangster*. He also captured the sensitive role of a single parent in *Tyler Perry's Daddy's Little Girls*.

Idris, whose father is from Sierra Leone and mother from Ghana, grew up in Hackney, East London. He spends much of his time with his daughter from a previous marriage.

Dear Idris:

I enjoy your work and was excited to see that you were involved in the *Saving Our Daughters* book series. I would like to know if you feel that bi-racial dating can affect the relationships kids have with their peers? Along those lines, when a person is considering who they want to date or eventually marry, do you think the shade of one's skin color weighs heavily in that decision?

Also what are your views about the daughters of single parents not being comfortable with who their parents are dating, and what do think that young women can do to avoid being in bad relationships?

Thank you,

A Concerned Reader

To Whom It May Concern:

In this day and age, bi-racial relationships are more common, especially in larger populated areas. However, it can affect a child, when one culture is preferred over the other. To prevent identity problems, exposure to both cultures is a key factor.

I believe people today are more attracted to physical appearance and social/career status rather than skin color. It's true, some people are narrow-minded and still have their preferences, but for the most part, I think color in relationships is a thing of the past.

When it comes to communication in the family, I have heard so many stories, where children were not open about uncomfortable situations and ended up sexually abused. Being a teenager and communicating with parents can be difficult, but boundaries need to be set in the beginning so there is an open line of communication.

Now when it comes to bad relationships, they are unhealthy at any age. A person in that situation needs to know that it is okay to leave. Often we get caught in the moment and tend to neglect what is truly best for us. Letting go may seem like the end of the world, but doing what's best for your future is most important.

Sincerely,

Idris Elba
...From A Man's Point Of View

"The only one you have to impress is God."

~ Rockmond Dunbar

Rockmond Dunbar has been named one of "Television's 50 Sexiest Stars of All Time" and is best known for his leading role as Kenny Chadway, the hard-working family man and entrepreneur on Showtime's critically-acclaimed drama series, *Soul Food*.

Another of his unforgettable roles was as the understanding father and husband in *Tyler Perry's The Family That Preys*, a film in which Sanaa Lathan plays the wife who disrespects him as a man, father, and husband. Seeing that character do what we could never imagine Kenny doing to a woman, evoked a huge response from audiences around the globe. He also stars in the hit Fox series *Prison Break*.

Dear Rockmond:

You are such an amazing actor, and I have heard that you are a gentleman. I would like to know about the leading women in your life that have inspired and influenced you to become the man you are, and do you think those ladies would be inspirational role models for young ladies today?

What do you think about interracial relationship, and do you feel that there is discrimination within the African-American community?

How did you prepare for your role in *The Family That Preys*? Was there anything special you did to get in the mood for your character and how did it feel lashing out on actress Sanaa Lathan in the movie? Also based on how your character responded, I want to know why men seem to be so angry against women?

How important do you think communication is to having a healthy relationship, whether it be as friends, family, work or any other type? Speaking of communication, how would you advise a young lady on getting out of a bad relationship, and how do you define a bad relationship? What qualities did you look for in a woman, and what qualities do you need to bring to the table in order to find that woman?

My final thoughts are about discipline. Do you think there are differences between the way African-American father's discipline and the way fathers of other cultures discipline, and what would you say to a young lady whose father is not in the home?

Thank you,

A Concerned Reader

To Whom It May Concern:

Well let me start by answering your first question. I would say definitely my mother, because my mother taught me the best. She gave me the values about how to be the best man I could possibly be. She instilled confidence and a passion in me. She gave me the ability to hold tenacity within my soul and never give up. She taught me how to fear God and why it's necessary, and she is number one on my list.

The second hero I have is my girlfriend Machico. I say that because she basically reinstated my love and passion for black women and for women in general. I went through a few devastating relationships, and she kind of just gave me back that faith and hope in true love and respect that's within a relationship. She challenges me to be a better person and to be a better man. She protects me and doesn't allow me to do stupid things.

I also have to say my grandmother. I have a strong affinity and love for her. She loved me so much and gave me a huge respect for why you should respect women. She was so strong and so compassionate. She was so compassionate that she allowed me to feel, you know. Within our culture, men, at times, are expected to be extremely masculine, and to our own detriment sometimes, black men are expected to be even more masculine. My grandmother allowed me to feel and she allowed me to explain my feelings and not feel judged. I've always appreciated her for that.

My Auntie Alma held me close. Auntie Alma cooked for me and always supported and gave me positive feedback, or she just tried to uplift me and lend a helping hand. She was always there and never let us down. She always wanted to help us do the right thing.

So those are my heroes. You have to choose people within your realm, I mean I could choose people outside of it and of my world, but those are the women who helped me exist and become the person I am today.

All of them should be influential because they walk with dignity. I think a lot of our young sisters out there today misconstrue what it means to be a lady. They give up their "ladyness" for no return. These women I mentioned earlier didn't compromise their integrity, their God or their dignity for anything, anyone or certainly any man.

There are so many young ladies out there today that I think are compromising their bodies, their minds, and/or their dignity for little or no return. So that's why I think they'd be positive role models. My Auntie Alma and my grandmother have passed away, but my mom and girlfriend are still here and they're very strong women who don't compromise their integrity. I think that's the most important thing.

In discussing interracial relationships, I really I think interracial relationships affect families and kids when people are coming from a negative place. You know, the ethnic side that says we must live, breathe, and eat the same thing. Education is the number one thing that plays either a good part or a bad part with an understanding of multi-racial relationships. There are people who feel we should just stick to our own race, be a part of our community because we walk and talk the same way and think the same.

You know what though, there are some brothers and sisters within this world that I don't share the same beliefs with, and there are those that I do believe in the same things that they believe in. There are some Caucasian, some Asian, and some Latino people that walk this earth that I'm in accord with. I could also be in accord with my brother who lives next door.

So the number one thing to understand is that we are all human. In a word, we are not all born and bred the same just because of the color of our skin. I never think that should be an issue.

One of my grandmothers was Italian. My girlfriend is a mix of Cherokee Indian, Caucasian, Japanese, and black, but we are black. We are African-American, and we are very proud of that. We are proud of our heritage and that dominates all. That's why I have a healthy respect for all. I consider myself to be a lover of all things.

I don't have a favorite color, nor do I have a favorite song. So, how could I just pick one thing? I used to have a tattoo on my back that was of all races of the world united together for brotherhood and I would rather stand for that than to just pick one race and say, "Let's just move forward." Because at the end of the day, it's just one big gang and gangs never win.

We should all pull together in this country and help one another because we're human. By doing that, we'd be so much better off than being separated and saying, "You're black so sit in this group and you're Asian so sit in that group," or, if we said, "Let's only help each other and not help across the board." We wouldn't get anywhere. You can see that if you look at every gang, and you can see that if you look at every religion, which as you know is another type of gang. It turns into a very difficult situation.

It would be a better world if you accept each other's ideas, you have healthy relationships, and you can communicate with one another. There should be love, and you have to be a lover of all things to have a healthy relationship within this world.

As black people, we discriminate and are so critical, and we're very critical of those within our own race. We're very judgmental. I know that, because I was born, bred, and raised within the black community. I cannot speak for any other community.

Let's go back to when I auditioned for *Soul Food*. I was twenty-five, and at that time Vanessa, who played my wife was, well I guess everyone knows her age now. She's eleven or twelve years my senior. Then we hired Aaron Meeks to play our son, and the boy was thirteen years old. Black people are so unforgiving. If they've seen the movie and no one believes I am the father of this thirteen-year-old boy and the husband of this older woman, they are going to say, "I know he ain't and there is no way I'm going to believe it."

Thank God I'm a decent actor and I actually pulled it off, but that was a huge fear that I had. Once we don't believe something, we are not willing to accept it, and that's something we do as a culture. We don't let something cultivate. We don't let something grow. We just beat it down and kill it at the very beginning.

Let something cultivate. Let something develop. We gossip too much and even without getting the entire story. I think we're like the *TMZ* (a celebrity gossip TV show) of a lot of races. Let's stop judging. Live your life to the best of your ability. Stop gossiping. Be more like God and be more like Jesus intended for you to be. It's in the Bible every day, and yet in every church you go to, you get gossipers. That's a very, very detrimental trait we have within the black community. I pray every day that we really squash it because it's not something that's serving us at all.

You asked about my role in *The Family That Preys*, and uh no, there was not anything I did special at all, I wouldn't say like in preparation. I had just come out of a relationship that was similar. I got divorced because I found out that my wife was cheating on me with another man, and a part of me felt like I was that character. It made me a little upset because I thought, "How could you be so naive?, and I wondered, "How could I be so stupid?"

I consider myself to be a very intelligent man, and not much gets by me. Right, but it was very introspective when Tyler gave me the role and I was like, "Wow. Does he know a part of my life that I didn't think that he knew?"

Of course, I didn't do the slap within my relationship. I'm definitely not an abuser. I can communicate, so I don't need to speak with my hands, but at that moment this guy has held on to and dealt with so much. So instead of communicating or trying to communicate or being able to communicate his feelings or his insecurities, he lashed out. You know some people get to that tipping point, and it's believable because it happens.

I was there watching the film with people, and they were cheering and yelling and screaming when I slapped Sanaa. It's so funny; I looked at it a little bit different. I remember I was walking through the grocery store and Michael Bart-Duncan came up to me -- we live in the same neighborhood -- and said, "Rockmond, man, I tell you brother, when you slapped Sanaa, I was like, yes!"

You know he's like the biggest dude since the biggest dude, but it's still domestic violence. He said, "I know man, and I would never put my hands on a woman, but she was taking you through it." That's a part of it too, regardless of the moment. That's another thing that we have to look at, retribution. God should be the only one with that "get back" power. "And this is mine," said the Lord.

So, to me that crosses the line, when in every situation it shouldn't have been cheered. It does happen in real life and I wish that it did not. Domestic violence can never, ever be right.

Yes, it can seem that men are very angry against women, Well, I try to go out and talk to young men and help them understand that we need to change this dynamic of this machismo thing that we have. We need to change the dynamic of handling everything in a masculine way, and change the idea of handling everything through violence and anger.

I also let them know that even if we changed that, we're still men, so no one can take that away from us. We need to handle situations in a more sensitive, direct way, and when I say sensitive, I'm not talking about in a female way of sensitive. I'm talking about with more understanding, with more compassion and more like Jesus, because who's to say that Jesus wasn't a man.

I think our women would respond to us in a different way. It would be so much more of a nurturing relationship than, "nigga, bitch, nigga, bitch." You know that. So let's find some other words in our vocabulary that we can use to express love versus, "What's up my nigga?" I know it's endearing, but I think it's now time that we stop. I think it's time that we've grown away from that, and it shouldn't be accepted anymore.

We need to relearn and redefine masculinity through sensitivity. We need to relearn that it's not cool to speak slang all the time and to relearn this idea of what healthy relationships are.

Unfortunately because it's been going on for so many generations, most families haven't been handing down what a healthy relationship is, what healthy communication is, what loving yourself really is or what respecting yourself really is.

It's not about wearing the flyest clothes, because that's not respecting yourself. "Oh yeah, I got my teeth done, son." That's not respecting yourself, that's not even taking care of yourself or loving yourself on the inside. The exterior can be totally different, but you have to understand how to take care of your mind and your soul because what you put in will definitely come out.

When it comes to all relationships we have, I think that communication is number one, and it has to be effective communication. That's the biggest thing. You have to be 100 percent committed to the relationship, and you can't be co-dependent. To me co-committed means being in a relationship where you're responsible for your own actions and feelings. You can't ever make someone feel a certain way. "You made me feel like this."

That can be interpreted and explained in so many different ways, because most of the time people don't really understand what the other person actually meant. Like a text message can be taken 1,500 different ways. Effective communication is so absolutely important. I believe there are so many different ways to say I love you and I hate you, but you can't cross the two.

You have to be very patient, understanding, willing to forgive, willing to understand, and allow someone to be human. That means, hey, look, I'm going to make mistakes from time to time. Sometimes I'm going to make mistakes. I'm going to think I'm right within that moment, but you have to allow me room for mistakes because I am human.

That doesn't mean, oh you hit me once and I'm going to allow you room to hit me like 500 more times. That's not what I'm saying. We're talking about words here. You have to be very cautious and think about what you say before you say it and not get too emotional.

Emotional communication never works. It never ever works.

You have to be very clear and understand what you're saying before you say it. I wish there was a class that we start off in grade school where we teach children to effectively communicate what they mean, what they're actually saying, and how people perceive it. Teach them how inflections and different tones can send off different messages.

"I just said I love you."

"But it's the way you said it."

"Well I'm saying I love you."

That just doesn't read love to me, and I just don't get it in that tone. You see what I'm saying? And that is what I think we have within our community too. It's this tone. At the end of the day, it sounds angry because it sounds angry for the most part, because I had to learn that growing up. It sounds like you're very combative and defensive.

I remember helping my mother with this very same thing. I'm like, "Mom, when you said this you sounded very defensive so I didn't know how to take it." Then she realized that she did say it kind of curtly. "So let me say it this way."

It gives that person the opportunity to reconnect again within the conversation. It's just very important. I think we fight to get our words out within our family, and that's where it begins.

So I think it's very important to take the time to effectively communicate with one another, and it doesn't necessarily mean you're some brainiac. You're just trying to take the time to let people know, "This is what I really mean."

My idea of a bad relationship is one filled with derogatory language, abusive language, being lied to, manipulated or deceived. One where you do not feel cared for or [do not] feel respected, and I do not mean from a selfish point of view.

If she doesn't feel that she is a part of the relationship, she needs to be in a relationship that allows her to feel her best. In a relationship, you should bring out the best in each other. If you're not, it's time to go, and I mean it's really time to go.

I'm not saying you can't have arguments, disagreements, or at times bring out the worst in each other, but know when to bring it back in and to complement each other. If the majority of the time you are bringing out the best in each other, then that's good, and it goes hand-in-hand with great communication.

There were a lot of qualities I looked for in a woman. I looked for someone who is intelligent, compassionate, and had high standards. I looked for someone who is one, not afraid of me, but also who is not afraid to be competitive with me. I also wanted someone who was attractive. There is no way we can have an intimate relationship, I don't care how small of one, if she's not attractive.

I've gone to college and I'm going to say this again, she had to have common sense. That's very, very important to me. You don't realize how important that is until you get into a relationship with a person who just doesn't have common sense, and you're like, "What was I thinking?"

I mean I need someone with common sense, someone with a sense of style, and someone who is God-fearing. I have a long list of qualities, and if you hit most of them, then you might be all right.

Cleanliness is a must, so someone who takes care of her body and her skin. She might have psoriasis, but if she is trying to take care of it, she's not just letting it take over her life. I would look for someone who is stable, and I'd want someone who thinks I'm the best thing since sliced bread. You have to dig me in order to be my woman. If not, we got a problem.

What I need to bring is stability, confidence, a God-fearing household, dependability, and I need to bring every bit of man that I can. I do not mean just a man that does it with authority, but who also does it with compassion and a great understanding of human nature.

I have to be intelligent, and I don't have to be a know-it-all, but I should know enough to do better than just getting by. I also have to be willing to learn, and not think that I know everything. I need to be confident, but not arrogant, and keep my ass cool too, because you got to keep it together.

I should also have a good appreciation and understanding of what my mate goes through being a woman.

It's really difficult to say if there are differences between the way African-American father's discipline compared to the way fathers of other cultures discipline. It's like, which crime in the United States is publicized more, the O.J. Simpson trial or Jeffrey Dahmer? I don't really know what to tell you.

I think and hope that fathers can do a hell of a lot better and that's been proven. I'm not going to single out Asian, Hispanic, Caucasian or African-American fathers. I'm just not going to do it. I'm going to single out all fathers and put them in a pool together. From what I have seen of men that have children in the United States, I say that we, even though I'm not a father yet, we've got to do a better job. We have got to do a hell of a lot better.

My advice for that young lady who doesn't have a father at home is that it is fine if it's someone in your life or if it's someone you can see from afar. Look for the image of the man you like, and look for someone who respects women and is intellectual. Try to find the healthiest image that you can possibly find in a man, and use that model for who you keep around you.

If you see that men are disrespecting women, you don't need to be around them because they're a negative image. Don't tolerate or put yourself in a position where you are compromising your dignity for any man. I would tell a young woman who doesn't have a father-figure in her life to pray for God to send you the best possible father-figure for you.

Pray for a man of dignity, a man of God, and pray for a man who can help you be the best possible woman you can be. I guarantee you that God will send that man for you and you will not question, "Is this him?"

I have one final thing I would like share to with our young girls. Be patient and don't be in a rush. There is so much that life is willing to give you. Try not to just go with the most popular thing. Try not to be within fads. Don't get caught up in gossip or rumors.

The only one you have to impress is God. The things that you are looking for, God has. Lean on God's shoulder, and He'll show you compassion. God has all the desires of your heart.

Sincerely,

Rockmond Dunbar
...From A Man's Point Of View

"I am a product of a bi-racial relationship and it taught me to respect all ethnicities..."

~ Boris Kodjoe

Boris Kodjoe is known for playing characters that always treat his opposite mate with the ultimate respect, making him an easy choice for participation in the Saving Our Daughters movement. He's had roles in films like *Love and Basketball*, *Brown Sugar*, *Tyler Perry's Madea's Family Reunion*, the upcoming sci-fi film *Surrogates* with Bruce Willis, and the popular Showtime series *Soul Food*. The former model speaks German, French, English, and Spanish fluently and is the owner of an online custom clothing company.

He was born in Vienna, Austria, to Ursula Kodjoe, a psychologist from Germany, and Eric Kodjoe, a physician from Ghana. Boris is married to his former Soul Food love interest, Nicole Ari Parker, with whom he has two children. Nicole and Boris are founders of Sophie's Voice Foundation, established to raise money for spina bifida, a condition their daughter was born with.

Dear Boris:

Boris, since the majority of your roles have been characters that exemplify treating woman with respect, I would like to know who are some of your favorite women role models and what is your viewpoint about bi-racial relationships and issues of color between men and women.

As a parent, how do you instill positive values in a daughter as it relates to her relationship with her boyfriend and setting up boundaries for her? What would you say if a young woman is in a bad relationship and needs to get out of it?

Now that you have children of your own what would be the one piece of advice would you provide a young lady who does not have a father at home and our last question is what words of fatherly wisdom would you provide girls transitioning into womanhood?

Thank you,

A Concerned Reader

To Whom It May Concern:

My wife Nicole Ari Parker is most certainly a great role model for young girls. She represents integrity, intelligence, success, confidence, grace, and beauty. She loves young people and spends a lot of time mentoring girls about establishing a positive self-image, being confident about who you are, and what you want, and she talks about the importance of education.

I am a product of a bi-racial relationship, and it taught me to respect all ethnicities and to view them as an opportunity to learn about other cultures and mentalities. We live in a world in which the U.S. president is of mixed-race heritage.

That has had an amazing impact on the subconscious of children across the world. Now they truly know that they can achieve anything they put their mind to. I also think the shade of one's character is more important than the shade of one's skin color.

As to postive relationships, a parent should have the kind of relationship with their daughter that encourages communication about everything, especially with their daughter's boyfriend. As a parent, if you do not approve of your daughter's boyfriend, you need to talk to your daughter about the reasons you don't approve and encourage a meeting with him.

Daughters, this might help your parent(s) to open up and give the boyfriend another chance. If not, maybe you should consider rethinking the relationship, because, as parents, they are probably concerned about your well-being.

If you are unhappy in your relationship or if there's any kind of abuse or disrespect going on, you need to move on. You should love yourself enough to never settle for less.

If there's no chance of any kind of relationship with the father, girls need to use other positive male influences in their inner-circle to engage with. Having positive communication with a male will remove negative perceptions and thoughts about men in general and establish a healthy self-image, without feeling the need to constantly look for the replacement daddy.

The fatherly wisdom I would provide girls is believe in the good in men and women alike. Don't be afraid to communicate with others and to show your strength and beauty. You are confident, and you are ready for the world. Make choices based on strength and not based on fear. Most of all, love yourself every day, and the rest will be a piece of cake.

Sincerely,

Boris Kodjoe
...From A Man's Point Of View

"Take a stance for what you believe in."

~ Columbus Short

C olumbus Keith Short, Jr. is an NAACP Image Award-winning actor for his role of Little Walter in *Cadillac Records*, appearing alongside Jeffrey Wright and Oscar winner Adrien Brody. He is also known for the lead role of D.J. in the motion picture *Stomp the Yard*.

Columbus has also appeared in the movie *This Christmas* also starring Chris Brown, Idris Elba, and Lauren London.

At the time of the interview, this married father of a young son was filming *Death at a Funeral*, a British comedy co-starring Chris Rock, Tracy Morgan, and Martin Lawrence.

Dear Columbus:

Thank you for the opportunity to write. I loved your work in *Stomp The Yard* and thought it was great that you were involved with this book series. I want to know if you would you mind reflecting on bi-racial relationships, and how you think they affect kids in the relationship?

Do you think some men are color blind more than women, and do women more than men sometimes make judgments of the person's skin in choosing their relationships to determine the shade of color of their unborn children?

What kind of advice would you give a young lady about talking to her single mother if she is uncomfortable with her mom's boyfriend, or if she is uncomfortable with the relationship between her own boyfriend and her mother and/or father? If a young woman is in a bad relationship and needs to get out of it, what would you tell her?

The last thing I would like to ask you about is what advice would you provide a young lady who does not have a father at home?

Thank you,

A Concerned Reader

To Whom It May Concern:

Bi-racial relationships . . . I believe we are all humans and it is our society that is kind of taking on the ideals that pigeons are with pigeons, dogs are with dogs, and cats are with cats type of mentality. But we are humans and we all believe the same, die the same, and wake up the same. So my opinion is that to each his own.

As far as how it affects kids, bi-racial children have a hard time I find because it is night and day to them. You're torn between two cultures and two worlds that our society is not one, so their place is kind of in a racial purgatory.

They find themselves struggling to fit in. I'm black but yet I'm white, I'm white yet I'm Asian or Japanese, and the gamut from there. It's tough on bi-racial kids. I really believe it is just tough to be a bi-racial kid.

On the topic of men or women being more color blind, absolutely men are more color blind than women. Most men only tend to think with below the pants. Women tend to think with their hearts, but I see lately, though, that women more than men are tending to stick with their own.

It's a weird thing. You're starting to see the black girls with the white men, the white women stand with a couple of brothers, but for the most part you see the sisters staying with brothers. It's kind of a weird thing that I never thought about before.

We're talking about these women vs. men things. Some people do and some people don't. It's a people thing, not women vs. men thing.

If a daughter is uncomfortable with her mom's boyfriend, then as a family these issues are important to discuss, because being uncomfortable and bottling it up will only create more issues later, so absolutely, it is important to discuss it.

The same thing applies to whomever you may be dating. If you're serious about this guy and it's not just something that is merely fleeting, if it's something that you want to take a stand for, then I say take a stance. Take a stance for what you believe in. It doesn't matter what age you are, I am an avid believer in that.

Now for women in bad relationships, they can put out an album. Nah, just kidding. It's easy to say just go, but there are a myriad of emotions that are attached in physical and mental abuse that tends to lend to insecurities and lack of confidence. So it's tough to just give that an answer, because I try not to, in anything, be looking in other people's backyards.

That's a tough one. I could not even begin to give advice on that because I have never been in that situation, nor will I, because I am not a woman and I haven't been battered so it's a tough one.

I have always said that if I have a daughter, I am going to love her better than anyone can love her. So when she gets out into the world, as soon as she hears, "Ah baby, you're fine," or, "Oh you look so pretty," she doesn't just fall apart. Instead she'll look at them and say, "Oh no, you're going to have to come at me with something better than that."

I see that when you find promiscuity in these young girls, right now, it's because they're fatherless. They weren't raised with the love of a father that was there. So my advice is to wait to be treated the way you deserve to be treated.

Some women do not know that they deserve to be treated like queens, with the utmost respect and dignity. You don't have to lower yourself or let down on any standards morally, spiritually, physically, mentally, and the whole gamut for someone saying, "You're pretty," or someone saying, "Oh, I love you and I'm going to give you the world." You deserve actions and not words.

I cannot really speak fatherly words of wisdom yet, because I am not a father to a young woman transitioning. I have a son, so I am trying to raise him up to be a gentleman. So when he runs into that girl we are talking about, he knows how to treat her and she knows how to be treated.

Sincerely,

Columbus Short
...From A Man's Point Of View

"I know the saying is that it takes a village to raise a child, but I want to know who is raising the village."

~ Gary Owen

Gary Owen's side-splitting comedy has entertained America for over a decade. He recently joined the cast of *Tyler Perry's House of Payne* as the new barber, Zach, after Perry met Owen on the *Tom Joyner Morning Show*. Owen can also be seen in the comedy films *Little Man* with the Wayans brothers, *Rebound* with Martin Lawrence, and *Daddy Day Care* with Eddie Murphy.

Owen continued doing stand-up in San Diego, and had a huge African-American fan base. He went on to win the "Funniest Black Comedian in San Diego" contest. Gary made history by being the only white male to host BET's *Comic View*. Gary and his wife (of African-American descent) have two children, whom he says are the coolest people he knows.

Dear Gary:

I love your comedy act and the work you have done on the *Tyler Perry's House of Payne* show. I am wondering who you consider to be your own female role models?

I understand that you are in a bi-racial relationship. Would you mind reflecting on it and others that are in one and how it may affect kids in the relationship? You discuss your family so lovingly, what drew you to your wife? How did your parents react to your bi-racial relationship and has that changed since you've given them grandchildren?

Many teen girls of single parent mothers are uncomfortable with their mom's boyfriend. Do you think that these daughters should discuss their feelings with their mothers and does it play a role in young women being in bad relationships?

I am really curious to know if you feel there is any difference between fathers of different ethnicities (African-American, Caucasian, European, Asian, Hispanic, etc.) when it comes to raising and disciplining children? Speaking of discipline, do you feel that it is appropriate for a father to spank his daughter, or should it be left to her mother? At what age does corporal discipline becomes inappropriate, and how do you feel about them taking corporal discipline out of the school system?

What kind of self-discipline should young ladies should have for themselves, and what expectations do you think a young lady should have for herself, her family, her community, etc.,? What advice would you provide a young lady without a father at home?

The last thing that I would like to ask you is what fatherly words of wisdom would you give girls transitioning to womanhood?

Thank you,

A Concerned Reader

To Whom It May Concern:

My wife is my female role model and that would probably be it, because I love how unselfish she is, especially the way that she puts her kids before herself. Growing up where I did in a trailer park near Cincinnati, OH, I did not see much of that. In fact, she has taught me more about putting our needs after others, in particular the needs of our kids.

You know, I thank God that she is my kid's mom, especially being a comic on the road. You can't put a price on the peace of mind I have knowing that my kids are safe at home with her.

You know, within the household there is not much to being in a bi-racial relationship, and my kids are not really aware of it. Even in school, which is a private school, they see a lot of diversity which was important to us when we were looking for a school to put them into. It just is not a topic of, "I'm black and you're not."

My kids are six and seven, and sometimes my daughter might notice that she is white (she's fair-skinned) and others are brown. She calls people brown and white, but neither of them distinguishes people as being different, so we have not had to deal with that yet.

You really want to know what drew me to my wife? She was hot, and that was my initial reaction to her, and she thought I was funny. We were actually friends for about a year before I asked her out.

There was one moment that I realized just how cool she was. I had just gotten home from being on the road about a week, and when she called to tell me she was coming over, I mentioned that I needed to get some detergent for the laundry I needed to do.

She surprised me when she showed up with the detergent. I just thought it was so cool that she would do that for me, even though she did not need to. That was a moment that really touched me, you know.

I am not close with my parents like that, so I wasn't worried about their reaction to my relationship. Dad and I are more like friends and Mom and I are close, but I'm not really concerned with their feelings about my relationship.

I would say without a question, that yeah a teenager should discuss being uncomfortable with her mom's boyfriend. There have been girls in my family who have had those moments and feelings about a mom's boyfriend, and it turned out that there were valid reasons to be concerned.

In fact, my wife did not let me meet her son until we had been dating for three months. Even then, she brought him by a comedy set I was working. She never let me see him at the house.

As a parent, it is important to realize that the example you set is the example your kids will follow. So if you are a single mother (or father) bringing different men (or women) in and out of the house for your kids to see, then you are setting them up to follow your behaviors later on in life.

If a young woman is in a bad relationship, she should get out, because it is not going to get better.

I can only speak for myself about any differences between fathers when it comes to raising and disciplining children. I think between me and my wife, we don't spank as often as we threaten to. My wife tends to whip them more than I do, because I usually can get by with the threat of whipping them.

You know, there was one time when we were at Denny's, and my son just would not heed the threats. So my wife took him into the bathroom, and you could just hear BOOM, BOOM, and BOOM.

My son came out with a look in his eyes that said it all, and from that moment on, my wife just has to look at him and say, "Do you remember Denny's?" Needless to say, the threat has firmly been established for my son.

Of course, when we whip our kids, it has to be constructive. We do talk to them about why they are getting whipped, and usually one good butt whipping is enough when they are little.

If both parents are in the house, I personally think that the mom should spank the daughter. I am just uncomfortable with the idea of spanking my daughter, even if I were a single parent, because it is too much like putting your hands on a woman. I do not want my daughter to ever feel that it is okay for a man to raise his hand to her or put his hands on her.

Eighteen is the age I think corporal discipline becomes inappropriate. I have been talking about one good butt whipping when they are little should do it, but you know when they get to thirteen or fourteen and think they are running stuff? It might be necessary to give them that whipping and remind them who is still in charge.

Nobody should hit or whip my kids besides me. In school, they do not love them, they may like them, but they do not love them and do not need to be putting their hands on them.

Now if someone else is raising the child, like grandparents or an aunt and uncle, I understand them giving a whipping, but again that is someone who loves the child and is doing it for the benefit of the child. If a principal or vice-principal is spanking my child, I do not know what kind of day they are having and whether or not they are going to take it out on my child.

When it comes to self-discipline and expectations, everyone while on Earth should want to do what they can to make it a better place while they are here. For young ladies, I think it is important for them to carry themselves in a way that commands respect. When they walk into a room, they should have a presence that puts out a good vibe, because people can pick up on that and will respond accordingly.

There's not much advice that you can give a daughter that is not your own. I know the saying is that it takes a village to raise a child, but I want to know who is raising the village. If there is not a father in the house, then the mom is really the one to show her daughter how to be. This means a mother cannot have men coming in and out of her house or allow others to disrespect her, because whatever her daughter sees is going to be the same actions that she will repeat as she grows up.

It's kind of cliché, but the words of wisdom I offer are respect yourself, respect your body, do not ever let a man call you out of your name (cuss you out), and walk away from uncomfortable situations.

Sincerely,

Gary Owen
...From A Man's Point Of View

"We must also work at communicating with them, and teach them about give and take in a relationship."

~ Chad L. Coleman

Chad L. Coleman is a veteran of the stage and small screen. Most people would recognize him as Dennis "Cutty" Wise from the critically claimed HBO series *The Wire*, but he has also made small screen appearances on *The Terminator: The Sarah Conner Chronicles*, *CSI: Miami*, *Life On Mars*, and will be in Fox's new fall release *Boldly Going Nowhere*.

Most recently, he was cast in the Broadway show *Joe Turner's Come and Gone*. As the father of an eight-year-old daughter, Coleman was excited to become a part of the Saving Our Daughters book series.

Dear Chad:

Thank you for taking the time to share with me, I would like to know who you consider to be your own female role models? Another question I have for you as a father is what do you think about bi-racial relationships and the affect they have on kids in that relationship?

I have several things that I would like to ask you about communication between parents and their daughters. First, should the teenage daughter of a single mother discuss being uncomfortable with her mom's boyfriend when she is, and what advice would you give this young lady about talking to them? What would you would tell a young woman that is in a bad relationship that she needs to get out of?

I would like to ask some things about discipline in the household. Do you think there are any differences between fathers of different ethnicities (African-American, Caucasian, European, Asian, Hispanic, etc., etc.) when it comes to raising and disciplining children? When it comes to corporal discipline, do you feel that it is appropriate for a father to spank his daughter, or should it be left to her mother only, and at what age do you think corporal discipline becomes inappropriate?

I also have some questions about self-discipline. What kind do you think young ladies should have for themselves, and what expectations do you think a young lady should have for herself, her family, her community, etc., and why? How would you define healthy boundaries for a young lady dealing with the opposite sex?

Could you share what advice would you provide a young lady who does not have a father at home?

I have a two-part question about relationships that a girl will have with boys. First, what qualities should a young lady be looking for in a boy that she is dating (and potentially considering for marriage as she gets older), and second, what qualities would you be looking for in a woman if you were in a position to develop a romantic relationship?

For my last question, what words of wisdom, as a father, would you give girls in their transition to womanhood?

Thank you,

A Concerned Reader

To Whom It May Concern:

I am happy to tell you who my female role models are. First and foremost, Lottie Byrd, my foster mother, and the woman who raised me, is a role model. She committed a profound act of selflessness by taking me and my two older brothers and sisters in and raising us up until my teenage years.

All of my sisters (Dee, Cheryl, Carol, and Angela) are role models for the unconditional love, forgiveness, and generosity of spirit that flows from them in their encouragement of me. Sally Stewart, the mother of my child, for being a strong woman of faith and character, and who unselfishly holds down the fort on a day-to-day basis in her unflinching desire to raise outstanding children.

In my marriage (though now separated), I have a stepson who is bi-racial. The main thing is to insure that the child equally identifies and internalizes the culture of both races, and though the mother/father bond with the child may not be evenly yoked, the child still completely sees him or herself fully realized in both races.

What I mean is identifying culturally or historically to the African-American experience. For example, when I talked to my stepson about how he identifies with being part French, he said the food and speaking the language.

When I asked him how he relates to the African-American experience, he was not as certain. So we discussed the Civil Rights movement, and how it was for his grandfather in the Korean War.

We talked about the fact that his grandfather lived during a time when segregation was a fact of life. We also talked about his grandfather's experience of the color barriers finally beginning to break down and [how] the inequalities he had grown up with began to decrease. As we spoke, my stepson began to identify personally with that part of his heritage.

Yes, a young lady has to try and communicate her feelings of discomfort with her mother, but if she runs into trouble, then she should seek outside help from a professional therapist, clergyman or trusted teacher.

If a young woman is in a bad relationship that she needs to get out of, she shouldn't blame herself or beat herself up about it. She should seek help from the above-mentioned to get the proper perspective on things she may be too young to see.

Yes, different cultures have different outlooks on corporal punishment. I'm not a student of this, but for instance in Thailand they still cane people, so you can only imagine that some of that is going to trickle down to how people raise their children. Some cultures believe women are inferior, so they domestically abuse them even though they don't consider it as such.

When it comes to discipline and spanking my daughter, I first must be a master teacher and communicator to my daughter. Now if I can't accomplish my goal of having her be a respectful and disciplined child through words or a look, then I won't hesitate to take it to another level to demonstrate that there are profound consequences to being willfully disobedient. That being said, by the time we get to her teenage years it should not be necessary to go there.

A young lady should expect unconditional love for herself, from herself, for her family and community, self-discipline, [and] healthy boundaries in her dealings with the opposite sex. [She should also have] an insatiable desire to learn, an unyielding love of God, and a desire to serve others.

From her family, she should expect unconditional love, support, guidance, encouragement, laughter, and a beautiful sense of belonging, acceptance, and security. She should also expect to be challenged cerebrally and inspirationally. Lastly, her family should make her feel like she can do anything she sets her mind to. From her community, she should expect respect because she'll carry herself in a manner that will oh so humbly demand it.

There are several ways that I would break down healthy boundaries for a young lady. First, she cannot put herself in compromising situations, and this also means staying in a safe environment where things cannot get out of hand. Next thing I would identify is that she should never use her body and sexuality to entice a young man into liking her, and she should also watch how she speaks to a young man.

In the same way that she should watch how she acts and speaks, she should also not be afraid to let boys know that sex is not an option. I want her to recognize that it is cool to be abstinent. It is also important to choose the right young ladies to be around. She needs to recognize that if she is rolling with the wrong kind of girls, then she is more likely to put herself into a compromising situation.

As I said earlier, they should find someone outside of their friends that they can trust talking with. It could be a professional therapist, clergyman or trusted teacher. I also highly recommend them seeking out a mentor who can help to guide them. They should not be afraid to find a way to email, call or text, in order to talk to them.

My advice for a young lady who does not have a father at home starts with saying don't allow the circumstance to draw you into victimization, feeling sorry for yourself or feeling less than anyone else. Become empowered by it and go out and start a support group for young ladies like yourself.

Find older women who have lived through similar circumstances and who are incredibly positive and strong, in spite of what may have occurred. You should also seek out a healthy male role model, preferably a man who loves God, himself, family, and community.

Wow, the first quality a young lady should be looking for that jumps out at me is that family foundation. Find a young man that has seen a healthy foundation on a daily basis and understands what it takes to have a healthy relationship between a man and woman. This is the first place that we all learn to be who we are. Anybody who has mommy or daddy issues is going to have issues in their relationships.

Unfortunately, women tend to find themselves drawn to the kind of drama that comes from these issues. It becomes very easy to be drawn into it, and it is not the key to a healthy relationship. If young women allow themselves to become enablers, then they are just asking for unhealthy problems in their relationships.

Young ladies should be looking for a young man who is not into alcohol or drugs at all. They should find a young man who is humble and yearns for continued learning. He should be a true gentleman who is respectful, not aggressive and knows how to treat a young lady. He should never put his hands on a woman, and he should be the kind of man that will open a young lady's door for her.

Look for a guy with a sense of humor and who doesn't take things too seriously, but he should have focus and passion for what he does. He must have goals and be working to obtain them.

Hmmm . . . qualities that I look for in a woman . . . She should be a woman completely comfortable in her own skin. She will be self-reliant, but she also appreciates and understands a co-partnership without being co-dependent. She doesn't embrace victimization, because that is not an empowering way to live. She is a woman who has dealt with herself honestly, in terms of her shortcomings and challenges as a human being.

She is a woman who really loves unconditionally and is strong in her love for God. She should be about internalizing the love she has for herself, the Lord, and those in her life. She should be about encouraging and building up people versus attacking their weaknesses and tearing them down.

She definitely must have a sense of humor and enjoy a good laugh. She must take care of her physical and spiritual health by being aware of what she puts in her body.

You know, as we discuss what young ladies should be looking for, as well as what I would look for, I would like to take a moment to reflect on this idea. As men, we have to realize that we are our daughter's first love.

That is the barometer by which they will measure a man's love, so we must be aware of how we show her love and teach them what unconditional love is. We must show them that there can be profound security from a man's love. We must also work at communicating with them, and teach them about give and take in a relationship. This is something that I make a conscious effort to do with my daughter every day.

For example, I took my daughter to a play today, and I made sure that I let her know how much I love her. It was little things like holding her hand and kissing her on the cheek and saying, "I love you." In return, she knew that it was okay to kiss my cheek back and let me know that she loved me too. When I talk to my daughter I always demonstrate the importance of respect and listening closely when she speaks to me, and that I expect the same behavior in return.

If we help them establish their own positive self-image and identity now, we can save them from society bringing down their esteem and confidence. Our daughters need to be able to tell people that they like themselves because their daddy has taught [them] the reality of their true beauty.

As a father, I would say to young ladies transitioning into adulthood to take your time and be patient with yourself. Trust the people around you who have always protected you, and don't let your friends and this capitalistic, "sell, sell, sell" driven society define who you are. Don't deny God's love, respect your body as a sacred temple, and be bold and fearless in your individuality, as long as it's tempered in spirit, and humility, and respect for all people.

Sincerely,

Chad L. Coleman
...From A Man's Point Of View

"Two people uniting, whatever color you are, is what life is all about."

~ E. Roger Mitchell

E. Roger Mitchell is a stage and film actor who may be most recognized for his role as the defense lawyer in *Tyler Perry's Daddy's Little Girls* where he defended the drug dealer Joe (played by actor Gary Sturgis, who also participated in Vol.1 of this book series).

He also appeared in *Tyler Perry's Diary of a Mad Black Woman* as Kalvin. Some of Mitchell's other films and tv shows include *The Faith of Men*, *The Driven*, *The Legend of Bagger Vance*, *The Shield*, *One Tree Hill*, and *NCIS*.

Dear E. Roger:

I am so excited for the opportunity to write you. The first thing that I would like to know is how do you feel bi-racial relationships are affecting our kids, families and communities, etc.? Another question I have is whether you think men are more color and culture-blind than women, and do you think we discriminate against each other within our own race?

When you were in school, what, if any, names were you called because of your darker skin color and how did you get through that? I would also like to know what advice you would give to young ladies missing a father at home?

In *Daddy's Little Girls*, you were Joe's attorney. Given the issues that character had, did you have any twinge of guilt based on who that character was? I know I have asked you a lot of things, but is there anything else you'd like to share with young ladies?

Thank you,

A Concerned Reader

To Whom It May Concern:

Your first question is pretty deep indeed. Well overall I will say, and this is my own personal opinion, that it's only a good thing when two people come together, regardless of whom they are. They take the time get to know and find out things about each other that they like or don't like, and they make the decision to be together. Two people uniting, whatever color you are, is what life is all about.

That's a beautiful thing, no matter what color you are. So that's how I feel about relationships in general, and that's how I deal with people in general, regardless of whatever you are. I don't look at it as interracial. It's just two people coming together.

So from that standpoint, I would imagine the love and the compassion that comes from the affection of two people deciding to be together and enjoy their lives together is all that matters. Based on that, I feel it should always be that way even if it is not necessarily the way it is. Relationships should be a positive thing, but then the color thing comes in.

If we look at the love and reasons that people come together, then who can judge that? No one can stand in judgment of anyone for loving a certain person, and if that person loves them, and they click together, then life is good. If they decide to have and create life together, that should also come from love. Unfortunately the society we live in chooses to make something out of it. So we'll look at it in that context, but it's up to the people who chose to have the relationship.

The husband and the wife, the mother and the daddy, regardless of their skin tones are the ones to pass along the communication to their young folk, their kids or whomever.

You know, just the basic morals of life. The next step is really up to the people. It's up to society. Society plays its part in things unfortunately, but that's when the people at home have to step up to the plate even more.

For me personally, I have two interracial nieces. I have a niece in DC. She is twenty-one years old and is a beautiful young lady. When I say beautiful, I specifically mean her spirit and who she is. She looks like us so she's beautiful. I also love her pop and my sister to death, and then my folks down in Tampa.

My other little niece is ten years old now, and she's growing up and is just as beautiful as she can be. So it's part of the American fabric. Look at President Obama and you can see how it is happening that we are evolving as a people in the United States.

I don't know if men are more culturally or color-blind. I think that just as men in general, let me put this out there. The way that a man looks at things as opposed to a woman, whether white, black or whatever, I think that men are a little more liberal.

In that regard, simply because a man is a man. A male is a male. Women you'll call us what ya'll call us. You've got a name for us, and some of us earn it and some of us don't. Sometimes it makes it bad for some of us who aren't as bad as others. We all possess those same qualities.

We are men, and we are wired differently than women. If there is a liberal or a more cerebral outlook, I think it boils down basically to male/female; we have Venus and we have Mars, and you know that they're two different planets.

That's something you can't really control, because sometimes it is complex and complicated. That'll be one of these things that'll be very interesting. It's a very good question. I don't know how to answer that one. I think it's just because we're men and they're women, and there are differences in that.

I'm glad you asked me about discriminating against each other within our own race. You know it's like we as a people, in our history and where we've come from, are doing a whole lot better, but there's still that individualistic, narcissistic kind of thing that we have.

I see it as the I/me/my way of doing things. I got me, I got to do me, and you do you. That's all very selfish, and I think it all stems from our cultural backgrounds. It's the separation of the family, not having the unity and not being able to come together and gather. I'm talking about four hundred years ago. I think we suffer from that. It's like I got a chance to get me somewhere, I'm going to get me somewhere, and I don't care about anyone else.

It's that thing where we sabotage each other, because we still have a little bit of that fear and self-hate. We definitely fear, and fear is no good for anybody. I personally think that there is a lot of stuff we have singled out.

There are artists out there like India Arie, who I love to death and who is a very close and dear friend of mine. She is just a wonderful person in my life. Just to give her a little something, something. She's singing about something that's positive. I think that our media and the music [are] very prevalent. It's powerful, and the things that we sing about and the things that we do also perpetuate problems that we have in our society as African-Americans.

When I was in school there was a name given to me because of my darker skin color. They called me black, and the person that dubbed me that name at that particular time was the most light-skinned, reddest Negro I'd ever known. Let me leave it at that, I won't call his name, but I was black and I loved it because I knew I was black.

My mother (Ms. Lou Ellen Mitchell), God bless and rest her soul, told me a little bit about that a long time ago. She said that the first thing that's going to come out of their mouth is, "You black so-and-so-and-so-and-so."

That's the first thing that's gonna come out when the s**t hits the fan. "You black so-and-so-and-so." It'll happen, and the chances of it happening are great. It's simply because of the visual man.

It's interesting how we don't call light-skinned people black so-and-so-and-so-and-so, because we just don't do that. Now that I think about it, it doesn't roll off of your tongue, but my mother said that a long time ago with only a sixth grade education.

I love her to death, and it's been eleven years since she passed away, but that's something from olden times, unfortunately. That example comes from something that old, and shows how we sabotage each other.

A young lady who doesn't have a father is somewhat at a loss, no matter how you cut it. If you don't have the male role model in your life, you're at a loss, somewhat, if you don't have Pops around to show you something that you should look for out there. That is what a daddy does.

Daddy's the guy that gives the young lady that mold that she should be striving for. You know, hopefully she compares the guy out there to her dad, who is a good guy and taking care of things.

So I would say if you don't have a father at home, hopefully there's somebody around that you can bounce things off of, you know, whether it be somebody else's dad, maybe a friend's dad or maybe a cousin's pop.

Joe from *Daddy's Little Girls* was something that definitely goes against who I am personally. You know, pretending to be a lawyer. It goes to the institution of law and how the law works. There are things that some lawyers tend to brush under the rug, and they have to put their feelings aside and do what pays the bills.

It's very, very unfortunate, and sometimes they could be defending someone who is completely guilty but that's their job and that's the choice that they made. For me personally, that's not how I am, but I know it exists in the world.

People make the decision to do these things. It is a part of the world that we live in, which is a very three-dimensional world. It's not all cookies and cream.

As an actor, it's a role, and I do it and I'm done. I try to do it as best I can so anybody whose looking gets a really, really good look at what actually exists in the world. It's all about reality and the imitation of life. So my job is to make that picture as crystal clear and as real as possible.

So yeah, I go down that road, but when I'm done, naw I can't live like that. That's not who I am. If I was a lawyer, I don't even know what kind I would be. I feel like I could be a lawyer, but I'm just saying that's not me.

There are some things that I would also like to share with young ladies. Young ladies, know that you are magnificent, you are wonderful, you are strong, you are beautiful, and you deserve the best. The best meaning is the one that you set for yourself, and not somebody else's definition of what the best is.

If you meet somebody and things meet your state, don't let someone else's definition of state dictate what you should do. You set your own expectations and your own boundaries. Shoot high, of course. At the end of the day when the lights go out and everybody goes home it's going to be you that is left with a person or without a person.

Nobody else can dictate that. It's up to you, but it's also good to confer or bounce things off people you trust. Take the meat, leave the bones, because you can listen, you can take in and you can talk to people and in the end you should only take what you need. Use it the way you need to, because at the end of the day, it's all you. Nobody else has to live inside your skin tomorrow. You wake up and it's you. Life is a compromise; a matter of give and take, but knowing that comes with maturity.

Talk about it, think about it, pray about it, and then make your decision. You want to always give your best. Life's a chance. It's no guarantee. So always do your best.

Sincerely,

E. Roger Mitchell
...From A Man's Point Of View

ACT III

TO WHOM IT MAY CONCERN
Reflections From The Women Of
Saving Our Daughters

Dear Reader - I leave you with this thought:

When someone teases, harasses or makes light of one's skin, he is belittling God and His work. God created everyone in His own image and, under the skin, we are all the same.

Each person should feel the pride of God's creation and we should each make the "finished product" a work of art and productivity.

~ Civil Rights Activist/Trumpet Awards Founder Ms. Xernona Clayton

Dear Reader - I leave you with this thought:

Be proud of who you ARE regardless of skin. How can anyone be proud of being white or pink or brown? It makes NO difference in terms of human value. What gives a person value is often how they value themselves. So be proud of your parents regardless of their problems. Find what you love in them, in you and be proud of that. Stop mean behavior everywhere. Try to be strong and loudly say "STOP!" when someone is mean.

Teach kindness and acceptance.

Open up and feel free to be who you are.

Play with everyone and don't judge anyone.

~ Actress Connie Nielsen

Dear Reader - I leave you with this thought:

As a dark skinned woman, my biggest discovery in life is that my beauty is defined not by the shade of my skin, but my love of God, my husband, family, embracing my dreams and ALWAYS loving, nurturing and respecting myself. It may sound like a "cliche," but when it is cultivated from within, people will SEE it.

~ Oscar Nominated Actress Viola Davis

Dear Reader - I leave you with this thought:

Why do you tease me because of the color of my skin? You tease me because you don't understand the history of this brown velvet skin that carries the burden of my ancestors and the triumphs of our sisters that fought for our Civil Rights. There is mystery associated with anything black. You tease me because of your ignorance and your parents' ignorance. It's not your fault; history has serviced your backwards thinking.

Times have changed. We live in a world where Black is running our country. President Obama has a white mother and African father. It's time for all races to appreciate our cultural differences and forge ahead united as one. There is no superior race. We are all children of God. We are all beautiful.

Walk with pride, stride, and dignity. It's time to achieve greatness! Black is proud, not loud. My young sister, be an image of all that is good and remember that your ancestors fought hard for you to have the freedom and equality that we are blessed with today.

Be a Phenomenal Woman like Maya Angelou. Black is indeed beautiful!

With all my love,

~ Actress Nia Long

Dear Reader - I leave you with this thought:

When I was in kindergarten, I attended a private school and I was the only African-American in my class. I definitely noticed right away that a majority of my classmates did not speak to me. When any of the kids passed out invitations to their birthday parties, I never received one, and that hurt a lot.

All I can say is you cannot change the color of your skin. Whether you are dark skinned or light skinned, love yourself, because self-love is more important than whether you are dark or light of skin. At least that is what my parents told me whenever I came home from school upset. So that is what I would tell other kids, learn to love yourself and all that other stuff will not matter.

~ Actress/Singer Keke Palmer

Dear Reader - I leave you with this thought:

Love yourself so much that you exude beauty, respect and graciousness & always be grateful for all the great & bad things in your life. Without the bad you can never learn how great to become.

~ Actress Tamala Jones

Dear Reader - I leave you with this thought:

When I was growing up, I was often teased about my weight, but I learned to ignore individuals who tried to upset me. Their power only lies in their ability to hurt, intimidate, and diminish others. Do not empower these bullies by letting them get to you. They are insecure themselves and make themselves feel better by teasing you.

Keep your head up and brush their dirty words away. You are the young queens of this Earth! Always remember that your beauty is infinite. You are the future wives, mothers, and nurturers of our culture and people.

~ Grammy Artist/Actress Jill Scott

Dear Reader - I leave you with this thought:

So much of being beautiful comes from within. The famous phrase "Beauty is in the eye of the beholder" means that everyone has a different opinion of what is beautiful. There's no way any one of us can be beautiful to all people.

When I find things to appreciate about myself I feel more beautiful. I feel beautiful when I'm working hard, when I'm sharing with others, when I'm laughing, when I'm eating a healthy meal, and when I'm noticing what's beautiful in others.

Beauty is an energy that can move in and out of our lives. It's not a stagnant thing. The more we pay attention to it, and find it in our daily lives, the more beautiful we will be. Also, just remember, in GOD's eyes we are ALL beautiful. :)

~ Actress Sanaa Lathan

Dear Reader - I leave you with this thought:

There are probably a few things that I would point out to the teen regardless of her age or environment. Hopefully I would have her undivided attention long enough to share a similar personal experience.

But most importantly, I would remind them that the most photographed and praised woman in this country right now, looks a lot like them (Michelle Obama). There is always going to be someone who has something negative to say about you. You decide and control how you're going to allow those things to affect you.

If Michelle Obama believed all the negative things said about her she would have not become a lawyer or a civil worker. I would explain that if she was not confident, she would not have been able to provide the support Senator Obama needed to become President. Like you, she endured teasing and other shortcomings but she made a choice. And because of that choice she has always succeeded. She continues to excel and influence positive change worldwide.

~ Actress Regina King

Dear Reader - I leave you with this thought:

Everything in life starts and ends with GOD the ALMIGHTY, and if you have and know GOD in your heart you know that He/She does not make mistakes!

You have to define your own beauty! Do not compare yourself to others. You are perfect just the way you are. When you embrace your own beauty, others around you will follow your LEAD!

Take your power back by KNOWING YOU ARE BEAUTIFUL NO MATTER WHAT THE SHADE OF YOUR SKIN IS!

~ Oscar Nominated Actress Taraji P. Henson

Dear Reader - I leave you with this thought:

A person who makes the conscious effort to ridicule someone for the shade of their skin is someone who has a very limited mind set. That person is unfortunately caught up in a time warp which will in the end not service their life mission as a whole. Transitioning from my acting career to my new passion of speaking to girls about financial literarcy was difficult. People said that my personality was TOO BIG and TOO COLORFUL. What I know is that "ALL OF ME" makes me special and unique. From the shade of my skin to everything else I have experienced in my life totally has gotten me where I am today.

Celebrate the shade of your skin because it is out of that skin that greatness will manifest. The road to overcoming being teased may be difficult, but it can be done. Whatever shade of brown you are, be it, love it, embrace it! Think on those things because they will service your mission in life and you will continue to blossom into the beautiful flower that you are.

~ Entrepreneur/Financial Coach Stacii Jae

Dear Reader - I leave you with this thought:

It is necessary for our young sisters and daughters to realize our greatness within. To represent ourselves in a way that honors our heritage and foreparents.

~ Actress/Singer Demetria McKinney

Dear Reader - I leave you with this thought:

Beauty is only skin deep! The color of your skin does not determine who you are or who you will become! When people tease you to make you feel bad, it's because they don't feel good about themselves. Never let words with no meaning bring you down. Black is beautiful! BELIEVE IT!

~ Author | TV Personality NeNe Leakes

Dear Reader - I leave you with this thought:

Affirm your daughter daily. Build up her confidence at home so the world will not be able to break her down. If she never hears from anyone else that she is beautiful, smart or capable, she should know she is all of those things because she hears it from you every day.

Speak into her life until you see her blossom into the strong, intelligent, empowered woman she was destined to become. Even when she begins to walk with her head held high, continue to affirm your daughter.

~ Actress/Entrepreneur Lisa Wu Hartwell

Dear Reader - I leave you with this thought:

God created you to HIS likeness. Love the skin you are in, you're beautiful, embrace it and don't let anyone tell you different.

~ Fashion Designer | TV Personality Sheree Whitfield

Dear Reader - I leave you with this thought:

Be proud of the color of your skin. God made you that color. He knew what He was doing when He did it. God does not make mistakes. You are wonderfully and fearfully made in the likeness and image of God.

Love the skin you are in. It is not the color or the skin that matters, but what you do with the gifts God gave you. How you use the skin that you are in to bring glory to God is all that matters.

Those who tease you do not like themselves. Love yourself just the way you are.

~ Judge Mablean

Dear Reader - I leave you with this thought:

It should be more of a compliment for people to tell you that you're smart or talented than for them to tell you anything about your physical appearance. Don't let someone undermine your worth, and understand that you hold the power.

It's such a mistake that so many young girls rely on their looks. Young women, we are all beautiful in our own ways...we must fight to not be one-dimensional.

~ Singer/Songwriter Keri Hilson

Dear Reader - I leave you with this thought:

God makes everyone perfect in his eyes, and when you love who you are, other people will too. People made fun of my color shade when I was younger, now it's one of the things people compliment me most about. It doesn't matter if people think you're too dark skinned, too light skinned, too olive or too pale; it makes you who you are and different and beautiful.

~ Actress Meagan Good

Dear Reader - I leave you with this thought:

You don't realize
   and it's right before your blue eyes
    how you have been brainwashed
      even hypnotized

by tv,
  video,
    picture show
     and other hoes
      to be similiar to the devils
       who ain't even on your level
        Trill things aren't weighed like gold

my SISTA the true jewel is your soul

~ Actress/Queen of Spoken Word Georgia Me

Dear Reader - I leave you with this thought:

You are beautiful because you are you.

Regardless of what other people look like or what clothes they are wearing, beauty is what is on the inside.

~ Actress Keshia Knight Pulliam

Dear Reader - I leave you with this thought:

Don't pay attention to anyone living in the past and color struck!

Baby, be proud of your skin hue because it is YOU! We come in all shades of color!

"That is SO old!" To anyone who has not advanced past skin color by now, WAKE UP!

It matters not what skin you're in. Everybody NEEDS some MOTHER LOVE now & then!

~ Mother Love

Dear Reader - I leave you with this thought:

We have to remember that kids can be cruel sometimes, especially when they don't have guidance in their lives. People come in all shapes, colors and personalities. You should not define yourself by someone else's standards. Every young lady needs to walk with their head held high, knowing who they are in their hearts and minds.

~ Actress, TV personality, and producer Alani "La La" Vazquez

Dear Reader - I leave you with this thought:

Concerning skin color, as a dark skinned girl, I LOVE my color but all my life people have been trying to convince me to hate it. But my opinion is the only one that matters because it's my skin, my face and my body. Skin color does not determine the validity of your heart. Beauty is so alive that it can not be diminished by any stipulations such as skin color, a scar or weight.

~ Actress Gabourey Sidibe

ENCORE

In Memory Of...

I will lift up mine eyes unto the hills, from whence cometh my help. My help cometh from the Lord, which made heaven and earth.

~ Psalm 121:1-2

"As fathers, we should lead by example as men and show our true love to our daughters on a daily basis. We should always insure our daughters about their beauty and never leave their side and protect them from the evils and disappoints of the world."

~ Author's Brother In-Law Eric Collins (In Loving Memory of his wife Tameika)

Heavenly Father,

Thank you for blessing our family with this miracle baby. I pray that you will give my brother the strength and support to love and teach baby Zarena and her siblings all that they need to know. Give them comfort when they long for their mother Tameika, who is resting with you now. Let his testimony bless all of our readers. In Jesus name we pray, Amen.

~ Author's Wife Debbie Collins-Benjamin

p. 177

"But He said to me, 'My grace is sufficient for you, for my power is made perfect in weakness.' Therefore I will boast all the more gladly about my weaknesses, in insults, in hardships, in persecutions, in difficulties. For when I am weak, then I am strong."

- 2 Corinthians 12:9-10

~ NOTES ~

~ NOTES ~

~ NOTES ~

LaVergne, TN USA
24 September 2009
158901LV00001B